The Blood of the Lamb of God

Larissa and Earle

I pray that the Lord Jesus may teach you through marriage relationship that we are in Union with Christ as our bridegroom and never separated from Him

Love in Jesus

Ahwini E. Verbeek

The Blood of the Lamb of God

A. Elizabeth Verbeek

Copyright © 2011 by A.Elizabeth Verbeek

Library of Congress Control Number: 2011901756
ISBN: Hardcover   978-1-4568-6279-4
              Softcover   978-1-4568-6278-7
              E book   978-1-4568-6280-0

All rights reserved. No part of this book may be reproduced or transmitted in any form or by any means, electronic or mechanical, including photocopying, recording, or by any information storage and retrieval system, without permission in writing from the copyright owner.

The cover art done by Jodi Verbeek from Verbeekdesign@comcast.net

This book was printed in the United States of America.

To order additional copies of this book, contact:
Xlibris Corporation
1-888-795-4274
www.Xlibris.com
Orders@Xlibris.com
91857

Contents

Introduction 9

Chapter 1   The Creation, the Fall, the Judgment,
and the Flood 13

Chapter 2   Covenant with Noah, Call of Abraham,
Covenant with Abraham, the Test of Abraham's
Faith, and Abraham's Faithfulness 22

Chapter 3   Israel's Deliverance through Moses, the Passover,
and the Purpose of the Law 28

Chapter 4   The Tabernacle of Moses, the Outer Court,
the Holy Place, the Most Holy Place, and the Ark ... 34

Chapter 5   The Sacrificial Offerings, the Priesthood,
and the Holy Garments of the High Priest 41

Chapter 6   The Day of Atonement, the Atoning Ministry,
the Feasts of Israel, the Weekly Sabbaths,
and the Holy Sabbaths 51

Chapter 7   The Prophesies Concerning the Lamb of God
from Old Testament and the Fulfillment of
It in the New Testament 58

Chapter 8   The New Covenant, the Passover Meal,
the Benefits of the Blood of Jesus, and
the Atoning Work of Jesus 74

Chapter 9   Reconciliation, the Spiritual Birth,
            the Revelation, and the Ministry
            of the Holy Spirit.. 80

Chapter 10 The Gospel of Grace, Paul's Revelation,
            Our Identification with Christ, Our Union
            with Christ, Rightly Dividing the Truth,
            and Communion with God,
            Personal Experience of God's Grace 87

Chapter 11 The Christian Pilgrimage, Christ is all
            and in all, Be transformed by the renewing
            of your mind, Why Christians Suffer?,
            Let us look at Jesus Christ... 98

Chapter 12 My personal experience of God's grace................... 109

Dedication

I submit this book at the feet of Jesus Christ for the glory of my Father in heaven who sent his Son to die for me and has revealed his Son in me as my only life.

I dedicate this book to my family I am blessed with: my husband Conrad, who is my constant help; my son Sanjay, who encourages me; my daughter-in-love Jodi, who supports me and my grandchildren, Emma and Olivia, who are a delight to me.

Introduction

I have often heard people say that they do not read the Bible because they do not understand it. Even Christians have made statements like the following:

"Why do we have to know all about Israel's worship system?"

"I do not understand the book of Leviticus."

"Jesus is okay, but I am terrified of the Old Testament God."

These statements sound like that of the Ethiopean eunuch who was reading from the book of Isaiah, Chapter 53, and wondering who the prophet was talking about (Acts 8:34).

Here in this book, I have tried to clarify some of the important things in the Old Testament that are types and shadows of the reality that was to come in the Person of Jesus Christ. I have also attempted to reveal the love of God for all humanity through Jesus Christ. Jesus Christ is God incarnated and walked among his people and talked about God's love and performed signs and wonders, including raising the dead, proving that he came from the other realm.

In the beginning was the Word, and the Word was with God, and the Word was God in the beginning. The Word became flesh and lived for awhile among us. We have seen His glory, the glory of the one and only Son, who came from the Father, full of grace and truth. (John 1:1, 14)

God showed his mercy and grace to all people through the life, death, burial, and resurrection of Jesus Christ.

The Bible is all about Jesus Christ from Genesis to Revelation. When you study the Bible, it will become more and more clear that the God and Father of our Lord Jesus Christ made his Son to be central in the universe.

> *Your attitude should be the same as that of Jesus Christ: Who, being in the very nature of God, did not consider equality with God something to be grasped, but made Himself nothing, taking the very nature of a servant, being made in human likeness. And being found in appearance as a man, He humbled Himself and became obedient to death even death on a cross! Therefore God exalted Him to the highest place and gave him the name that is above every name, that at the name of Jesus every knee should bow, in heaven and on earth and under the earth, and every tongue confess that Jesus Christ is Lord to the glory of the Father. (Phil. 2:5-11)*

If this does not make your knees tremble, I do not know what will. Jesus Christ is the Supreme Being in the universe.

> *He is the image of the invisible God, the firstborn over all creation. For by Him all things were created: things in heaven and on earth, visible and invisible, whether thrones or powers or rulers or authorities; all things were created by Him and for Him. He is before all things, and in Him all things hold together. And He is the Head of the body, the church; He is the beginning and the firstborn from among the dead, so that in everything He might have supremacy. For God was pleased to have all his [God's] fullness dwell in Him [Christ] and through Him [Christ] to reconcile to Himself [God] all things, whether things on earth or things in heaven, by making peace through His [Jesus's] blood, shed on the cross. (Col. 1:15-20, author's translation added)*

My prayer for the believers are that the God of our Lord Jesus Christ may grant us the spirit of wisdom and revelation in the knowledge of Christ, by having the eyes of our heart flooded with light, so that we may know and understand the hope to which he has called us. We are called to have fellowship with God. We have an organic union with God through Christ Jesus (John 15:5). The fullness of Godhead lives in Christ and we have been given fullness in Christ, who is the head of all power and authority (Col. 2:9-10). We have been raised with Christ and seated with Christ at the right hand of God (Col. 3:1). We must live out from the realm of Christ. Our hope is that when Christ, who is our life, appears, then we too will appear with him in glory (Col. 3:4). To the rest of you, I say that it does not matter what religion you are associated with. If you do not have Jesus Christ, you do not have life. Life is in the Son of God. Without life, you are incomplete and already stand condemned (John 3:18) to eternal death, which means permanent separation from the presence of God. My prayer is that everyone may be informed of the truth and be able to make the wise choice to have eternal life. If you choose to have nothing to do with Jesus Christ, for whatever reason, then you must understand the consequence. God desires for all to have life in Christ. God sent his Son to the world to die for us, thereby saying, "I love you and care about you." If we reject his free gift of life through Christ, then there is no more salvation left. The only one sending you to hell is yourself by choosing to go there by your own determination with the knowledge or in ignorance of the truth. We must never blindly follow any god because of our ancestors, traditions, or the pride in our own religion. We all must search the truth individually. At some point in life, we must all ask the question, "Who am I? Why am I here? What is the purpose of my existence?" You may ask, "What is the truth?" Only one person in the entire human history ever claimed to be the truth. Jesus said, "I am the Way and the Truth and the Life" (John 14:6).

God said that he has set before us life and death, blessings and curses but to choose life, so that we and our children may live (Deut. 30:19). The choice must be made while you are still in this body. It is the most important decision you can ever make.

Chapter 1

The Bible is a book of history, science, poetry, proverbs, wisdom, parables, and prophecy. The Bible teaches about the creation of mankind and the redemption of mankind. The Bible is also a book of moral and spiritual lessons. Above all the Bible is a testimony of Jesus Christ, who is the source of eternal life for all mankind. It is divided into two sections, the Old Testament and the New Testament. The New Testament is concealed in the Old Testament. The Old Testament is revealed in the New Testament.

> *It is the glory of God to conceal a matter; to search out a matter is the glory of kings. (Prov. 25:2)*

God created man and wrote a book to show us to live according to His principles.

> *All scripture is God-breathed and is useful for teaching, rebuking, correcting and training in righteousness, so that man of God may be thoroughly equipped for every good work. (2 Tim. 3:16)*

To understand the Bible, one must be born from above by the Spirit of God.

> *The man without the Spirit does not accept the things that come from the Spirit of God, for they are foolishness to him, and he cannot understand them, because they are spiritually discerned. (1 Cor. 2:14)*

The whole Bible is centered around Jesus Christ, the Son of God. Not only the Bible, but the whole universe is created by Jesus Christ for himself.

> *He is before all things, and in Him all things hold together.*
> *(Col. 1:17)*

God made Jesus to be the Supreme Being in the entire universe.

> *For God was pleased to have all his fulness dwell in Him [Jesus] and through Him to reconcile to himself [to God] all things, whether things on earth or things in heaven, by making peace through His blood, shed on the cross. (Col. 1:19, author's translation added)*

Therefore, if you are serious about studying the Bible, come on, let us look into it with the help of the Holy Spirit, and let us learn together of *Christ the Lamb of God, who was and is and is to come.*

The Perfect World

In the beginning, whenever the beginning was, God created the perfect world. God himself said it was very good (Gen. 1-3).

The story of creation goes like this:

And God said, "Let there be light," and there was light. God saw that the light was good and he separated the light from darkness.
 And God said, "Let there be an expanse between the waters to separate water from water."
 And God said, "Let the water under the sky be gathered to one place, and let dry ground appear." God called the dry ground "land," and the gathered waters he called "seas." And God saw that it was good.
 Then God said, "Let the land produce vegetation: seed bearing plants and trees on the land that bear fruit with seed in

it according to their own kinds." The land produced vegetation, plants bearing seed according to their kinds and trees bearing fruit with seed in it according to their kind. And God saw that it was good.

And God said, "Let there be lights in the expanse of the sky to separate the day from the night, and let them serve as signs to mark seasons and days and years, and let them be lights in the expanse of the sky to give light on the earth."

And God saw all that he had made and it was good.

And God said, "Let the water teem with living creatures, and let the birds fly above the earth across the expanse of the sky. And God saw that it was good. God blessed them and said, 'Be fruitful and increase in number and fill the waters in the seas, and let the birds increase on the earth.'"

And God said, "Let the land produce living creatures according to their kinds: livestock, creatures that move along the ground, and wild animals, each according to its kind." And God saw that it was good.

Then God said, "Let us make man in our image, in our likeness (notice the use of 'us', referring to the Triune God—God the Father, God the Son, and God the Holy Spirit), and let them rule over the fish of the sea and the birds of the air, over the livestock, over all the earth, and over all the creatures that move along the ground."

And the Lord God formed man from the dust of the ground and breathed into his nostrils the breath of life, and man became a living soul. (Gen. 2:7)

Notice that man was a living soul. There is no mention of the spirit of man in this creation account. God had planned in eternity past to indwell himself and become man's spirit in fullness. God himself would complete the man and make him fully tripartite.

God placed man in the Garden of Eden. God made all kinds of trees grow out of the ground—trees that were pleasing to the eye and good for food.

In the middle of the garden were the tree of life and the tree of the knowledge of good and evil.

And the Lord God commanded the man, "You are free to eat from any tree in the garden, but you must not eat from the tree of the knowledge of good and evil, for the day you eat of it you surely will die." (Gen. 3:3)

*God saw all that he had made, and it was very good.
(Gen. 1:31)*

Creation of a helper

The Lord God said, "It was not good for man to be alone. I will make a helper suitable for him. So the Lord God caused the man to fall into sleep; and while he was sleeping, He took one of the ribs from man and closed up the place with flesh. Then the Lord God made a woman from the part He had taken out of the man." Then the man said, "This is now bone of my bones and flesh of my flesh; she shall be called woman for she was taken out of man."

For this reason, a man will leave his father and mother and be united to his wife, and they will become one flesh. (Gen. 2:26)

The first couple was very happy and enjoyed everything God created. Adam and Eve had been given authority over all the earth. They also enjoyed the company of God and walked and talked with God in the garden in the cool of the day. This was the perfect world in every way.

The test of man's will

Man was created with a will to make his own choice. For this reason, God provided him with contrast to choose from the two trees. The tree of life is a type of the Lord Jesus Christ, God's eternal life source for man. Jesus said, "I Am the Life" (John 14:6). The tree of the knowledge of good and evil, on the other hand, will produce death.

The day you eat of it you surely will die. (Gen. 2:17)

Satan came to Eve in the form of a serpent and motivated Eve to *question* God's Word and said, "Has God indeed said, 'You shall not eat of every tree of the Garden?'" (Gen. 3:1) Eve *misquotes* God's Word back to Satan by saying, "Of the fruit of the tree of knowledge of good and evil, you shall not eat it, nor shall you touch it lest you die" (Gen. 3:3). God did not say not to touch the fruit. At this point, Satan deceives Eve by saying, "You shall not surely die. For God knows that in the day you eat of it your eyes will be opened and you will be like God, knowing good and evil" (Gen. 3:4b, 5). Satan, himself the liar and deceiver, used the lust of the flesh, the lust of the eye, and the pride of life to tempt Eve to transgress against God's Word. When Eve believed Satan's word, she ate the fruit of the *knowledge of good and evil.* Eve gave the fruit to Adam, and he ate of the fruit (Gen. 3:6). The Word of God says, "The eyes of both of them were opened, and they knew they were naked, they made covering for themselves with fig leaves" (Gen. 3:7). The covering with the fig leaf was man's effort to look right in the presence of God. This was the origin of religion, man's effort to approach God.

You might wonder at this point who Satan is and where did he come from? Let me take you to the origin of Satan. Here it is:

> *The word of the Lord came to me: Son of man take a lament concerning the king of Tyre and say to him: This is what the Sovereign Lord says: "You were the model of perfection, full of wisdom and perfect in beauty. You were in Eden in the garden of God; every precious stone adorned you: ruby topaz and emerald, chrysolite, onyx and jasper, saphire and beryl. Your settings and mountings were made of gold; on the day you were created they were prepared. You were anointed as a guardian cherub, for so I ordained you. You were on the Holy mount of God; you walked among the fiery stones. You were blameless in your ways from the day you were created till wickedness was found in you. So I drove you in disgrace from the mount of God, and I expelled you, O guardian cherub from among the fiery stones. Your heart became proud on account of your beauty, and you corrupted your wisdom because of your splender." (Ezek. 28:11-15, 17)*

How you have fallen from heaven, O morning star son of the dawn! You have been cast down to the earth, you who once laid low the nations! You said in your heart, "I will ascend to heaven; I will raise my throne above the stars of God; I will sit enthroned on the mount of assembly, on the utmost heights of the sacred mountain. I will ascend above the tops of the clouds; I will make myself like the Most High But you are brought down to the grave, to the depths of the pit." (Isa. 14:12-15)

Satan was Lucifer, the son of the dawn, created by God. Pride caused him to fall from the grace of God, and his name was changed from Lucifer to Satan (deceiver, prince of darkness). This was the first fall, and because Adam believed Satan above the Word of God, he too had to join company with Satan.

The fallen man and the consequences

God appeared in the garden. The Lord God called to the man. Adam answered and said, "I heard you in the garden, and I was afraid because I was naked; so I hid." (Gen. 3:10)

God questioned the man, "Have you eaten from the tree that I commanded you not to eat from?"

The man said, "The woman you put here with me, she gave me some fruit from the tree, and I ate it." (Gen. 3:12)

Then the Lord God said to the woman, "What is this you have done?"

The woman said, "The serpent deceived me, and I ate." (Gen. 3:13)

So the Lord God said to the serpent, "Because you have done this; Cursed are you above all the livestock and all the wild animals, you will crawl on your belly and you will eat dust all the days of your life. And I will put enmity between you and the woman, and between your seed and hers; he will crush your head, and you will strike his heel." (Gen. 3:14-15)

To the woman, he said, "I will greatly increase your pain in child bearing; with pain you give birth to children. Your desire will be for your husband, and he will rule over you." (Gen. 3:16)

To Adam, God said, "Because you listened to your wife and ate from the tree about which I commanded you, 'You must not eat of it,' Cursed is the ground because of you; through painful toil you will eat of it all the days of your life.

It will produce thorns and thistles for you, and you will eat the plants of the field. By the sweat of your brow you will eat your food until you return to the ground, since from it you were taken; for dust you are and to dust you will return." (Gen. 3:17-19)

The court session was over. Adam and his wife were judged and the serpent was cursed and the earth was also cursed by the Lord God. Adam tried to defend by blaming his wife, and Eve put the blame where it belonged with Satan.

What happened to the perfect family?

The moment they believed Satan's words against God's Word and acted upon by eating the fruit, they received the sin nature of Satan. What is the sin nature?

> *The acts of sinful nature are obvious: sexual immorality, impurity, and debauchery; idolatry, and witchcraft; hatred, discord, jealousy, fits of rage, selfish ambition, dissensions, factions and envy drunkenness, orgies and the like. (Gal. 5:19)*

This was the fall of Adam and the original sin, which was passed upon all men.

> *Therefore, just as through one man sin entered the world, and death spread to all men, because all sinned. (Rom. 5:12)*

While Eve was deceived into transgression, Adam was not deceived. God held him responsible for the sin and the fall of man (1 Tim. 2:14). This was also the origin of dysfunctional families on the earth.

> *The Lord God made garments of skin for Adam and his wife and clothed them. (Gen. 3:21)*

This is the evidence that man-made fig-leaf coverings were not acceptable before God. God moved in grace to deal with man's sin and provided an acceptable covering. An animal was sacrificed, blood was shed, for the covering of man's sin. God introduced a substitutionary sacrificial death in order to cover man's sin. The innocent died for the guilty. Life came out of death. This was the first animal sacrifice that pointed to the body and blood of the Lord Jesus Christ. (Heb. 10:1-12)

> *So the Lord God banished him from the Garden of Eden to work the ground from which he had been taken. After he drove the man out, He placed on the east side of the Garden of Eden cherubim and a flaming sword flashing back and forth to guard the way of the Tree of life. (Gen. 3:23)*

After the incident, God denied Adam access to the tree of life. They were banished from the presence of God. Death initially came to Adam's soul, and Adam received a spirit of fear, sin nature of Satan, and subsequently physical death.

God's chase after mankind

As you will see, God might have banished mankind from his presence but never stopped chasing them because of his unending love for them. God created mankind to have fellowship with them and to love and to be loved. God always has the Last Word because He had a plan from before the beginning of time.

As men began to increase in the world, the wickedness of men became great.

> *The Lord was grieved that He had made man on the earth, and His heart was filled with pain. So the Lord said, "I will wipe mankind whom I have created from the face of the earth." (Gen. 6:6-7)*

But a man called Noah found favor with God. The Bible says that Noah was righteous and blameless among the people and that Noah walked in obedience to God. God instructed Noah to make an Ark, and he and his family along with a pair of every kind of animals went into the ark. Then God destroyed the wicked people with the flood. Noah preached for 120 years about the coming destruction, but no one paid any attention until it was too late. The ark is a type of Jesus Christ. Today, like Noah, men and women everywhere proclaim the Word of reconciliation to God through Jesus Christ. Death and destruction is on the way. In Christ is our salvation and safety. By believing in him, you enter into the eternal ark of protection. But as in the days of Noah, the message has been dismissed and ridiculed by many in the world.

Chapter 2

After the flood, God made a covenant with Noah. A covenant is a binding agreement between two parties, one being the greater and the other lesser. By definition, it is an agreement to 'cut covenant' by shedding of blood and walking between the pieces of flesh.

> *Then God said to Noah be fruitful and increase in number; multiply on earth and increase upon it. God established His covenant with Noah and his descendants after him and with every living creature that was with him, that came out of the ark. (Gen. 9:7-10)*

The rainbow was the sign of the covenant. God said that whenever the rainbow appears in the clouds, he will see and remember his covenant, and the earth will not be destroyed by flood again. (Gen. 9:13, 14, 15)

The earth was once again populated by Noah's descendants. Wickedness continued on earth because of man's sin nature, the selfish ambitions. God saw that man's unified rebellion will soon deserve universal judgment. God stepped into the scene, at the tower of Babel and brought their unity into confusion, by confusing their language, scattering them on earth, and dividing them into nations. People continued to worship God's creation (sun, moon, stars, and idols carved out of wood) rather than God. At that time, God began to unfold his redemptive plan for the nations. God chose the next covenant man, from the line of Shem, one of the sons of Noah.

The Call of Abram

The Lord had said to Abram, "Leave your country, your people and your fathers household and go to the land I will show you." (Gen. 12:1)

Personal blessings to Abram are as follows:

I will make you into a great nation and I will bless you;
I will make your name great, and you will be a blessing.
I will bless those who bless you;
And whoever curses you I will curse;
And all people on earth will be blessed through you. (Gen. 12:2-4)

Abram had to leave his idols and his pagan household and go to a country God would show him.

God made a blood covenant with Abram. A blood covenant between two parties is the most solemn, the most sacred, and the most enduring of all contracts. When you enter into blood covenant with someone, you promise to give them your life, your love, and your protection forever.

The promise of the covenant was an extension of the covenants God made with Adam and Noah.

This covenant was not only made with Abram, but its oath was given to Isaac and was confirmed to Jacob and the twelve tribes of Israel after him. (1 Chron. 16:15-17)

God's covenant with Abram

After this, the word came to Abram in a vision, "Do not be afraid, Abram. I am your shield, your very great reward." (Gen. 15:1)

Abram complained about not having a child and that his servant will inherit all his possession. Then the word of the Lord came to him, "This man will not be your heir, but a son coming from your own body will be your heir." God took him outside and said, "Look at the heavens and count the stars if indeed you can count them." Then God said to him, "So shall your offspring be." Then Abram believed the Lord and the Lord credited it to him as righteousness. God also said to him, "I AM the Lord, who brought you out of Ur of the Chaldeans to give you this land to take possession of it." (Gen. 15:1-7)

Abram asked God how he can know that he will gain possession of it. So the Lord said to him, "Bring me a heifer, a goat and a ram, each three years old, along with a dove and a young pigeon." (Gen. 15:8, 9) Abram brought all these to God, cut them in two, and arranged the halves opposite each other; the birds, however, he did not cut in half.

As the sun was setting, Abram fell into a deep sleep, and a thick and dreadful darkness came over him, then the Lord said to him, "Know for certain that your descendants will be strangers in a country not their own, and they will be enslaved and mistreated four hundred years. But I will punish the nation they serve as slaves, and afterward they will come out with great possessions. When the sun had set and darkness had fallen, a smoking fire pot with a blazing torch appeared and passed between the pieces." On that day the Lord made a covenant with Abram and said, "To your descendants I give this land, from the river of Egypt to the great river, the Euphrates the land of the Kenites, Kenizzites, Kadomonites, Hittites, Perizzites, Rephaites, Amorites, Canaanites Girgashites and Jebusites." (Gen. 15:12-20)

God says, "Abram, I am your shield. I will protect you and fight your battles for you. I will be your strength. If any one attacks you, they are attacking Me. Your battles are mine. And when you go into battle, I will fight for you. You stand beside Me and let me do it for you."

The seal of the covenant

The covenant with Abram was called the covenant of circumcision because the covenant was sealed with the rite of circumcision (Acts 7:8). When Abram was ninety-nine years old, the Lord appeared to him and said, "I Am God Almighty; walk before me and be blameless. I will confirm my covenant between Me and you. As for me, this is my covenant with you: You will be the father of many nations. No longer you will be called Abram;

your name will be called 'Abraham' for I have made you father of many nations. I will make nations of you, many nations and kings will come out of you. I will establish my covenant as an everlasting covenant between me and you and your descendants after you for the generations to come, to be your God and the God of your descendants after you" This is my covenant with you and your descendants after you, the covenant you are to keep: Every male among you shall be circumcised. You are to undergo circumcision, and it will be the sign of the covenant between Me and you. My covenant in your flesh is to be an everlasting covenant. (Gen. 17:1-8, 10, 13)

The rite of circumcision was so important that no Israelite or strangers could partake of the Passover Feast unless they had the seal of circumcision. (Exod. 2:23-25)

God also said to Abraham, "As for Sarai your wife, you are no longer to call her Sarai; her name will be Sarah. I will bless her and will surely give you a son by her. I will bless her so that she will be the mother of nations; kings of people will come from her. (Gen. 17:15, 16)

The history of Israel shows that all these promises are fulfilled. Today Abraham is known as the father of Jews, Christians and Muslims.

The test of Abraham's faith

Abraham had a son earlier by Sarah's hand-maiden, Hagar. His name was Ismael. But the promised seed was to come through Sarah. Abraham was one hundred years old and Sarah was ninety, way past the child-bearing age. The birth of a son for this couple must be supernatural. Abraham began to understand and was fully persuaded that God is bound by his covenant and since God is God, he is able to keep his word. So a son was born to Abraham through Sarah as promised by God, and he was named Isaac (Gen. 21:5).

Now God was ready to test Abraham's faithfulness to the covenant. When a covenant is cut, each party surrenders himself in loving trust to the other party. He must be willing to give his total life and heart to the one he is in covenant with. It is a total surrender to the one you are in covenant with. The blood covenant is a binding agreement forever.

There was only one way to test Abraham's commitment to the covenant. God asked for that which was dear to Abraham, his son Isaac.

Abraham take your son, Isaac, your only son whom you love. Take him to the land of Moriah and offer him to me as a burnt offering on one of the mountains. (Gen. 22:2)

On the third day of the journey, Abraham looked up and saw the place in the distance. He said to the servants, "Stay here with the donkey while I and the boy go and worship the Lord and we will be back to you." (Gen. 22:5) Abraham believed that God is committed to his covenant, and that they will be back.

Then Abraham placed the wood for the burnt offering on his son Isaac. As the two of them traveled to the mountain, Isaac turned to Abraham and said, "Father, we have the wood and the fire, but where is the lamb for the sacrifice?" Abraham answers, "God Himself will provide the lamb for the burnt offering, my son." (Gen. 22:8) From this statement, we can understand that Abraham believed God would provide a substitute sacrifice on his behalf. Abraham believed that God could raise Isaac from dead and fulfill the promise God had made to Abraham about the firstborn of the covenant children. Abraham builds an altar and placed Isaac on it. Just as he was about to take the life of Isaac, God appears and says, "Abraham, now I know that you fear God, because you have not withheld your son, your only son from me."

Abraham found a ram God provided as substitute for Isaac and sacrificed it as a burnt offering.

Abraham's faithfulness

We read in Galatians 3:6 that Abraham believed God, and it was credited to him as righteousness.

Abraham believed God when he said to Abraham that he will have a son through Sarah, even though he was one hundred years old. Isaac's birth was a supernatural birth.

Abraham believed God enough to offer Isaac his son as a sacrifice.

Abraham believed God would provide a substitute or raise his son from the dead. Because Abraham believed God, it was credited to him as righteousness. It was God's grace, and all Abraham did was believe in God's Word. Because of this, Abraham is known as a friend of God. God is known as the God of Abraham, Isaac, and Jacob, who are descendants of Abraham.

Isaac was a type of Jesus Christ, the beloved Son of God, who was supernaturally born, "the Lamb of God," as a substitute who will take away the sins of the world.

Paul writes in Romans 9:8 that not all Abraham's children are the children of God, but only those who believe the promise God made to Abraham of the salvation, which was to come through Abraham's seed.

Jesus Christ in his humanity came from Abraham's lineage. (Matt. 1:1)

Thus the promise God made to Abraham that "all people on earth shall be blessed through you" (Gen. 12:3) was fulfilled in Christ Jesus with the New Covenant.

In the New Covenant, God is asking us to do the same thing he asked Abraham in the Old Covenant—to believe. God is asking us to believe that Christ the Son of God has entered into a covenant with God the Father on our behalf. We are separated from God, and nothing we can do to be righteous in the sight of God, unless we believe in the sacrificial offering of Christ as the Lamb of God.

God continued to chase humanity in his eternal love to bring them to be in his presence.

Chapter 3

Israel's Deliverance from Egypt

Just as God said to Abraham, the descendants of Abraham became captive in Egypt. They were in Egypt for 400 years and heavily oppressed by the Egyptians (Gen. 15:13-36). The cry of the people of Israel came up to God. God remembered the covenant he made with Abraham and Isaac and Jacob (Exod. 2:23, 24). God appeared to Moses and said:

> "I Am the God of your father, the God of Abraham, the God of Isaac and the God of Jacob" Then the Lord said. "I have indeed seen the misery of my people in Egypt. I have heard them crying out because of their slave drivers, and I am concerned about their suffering. So I have come down to rescue them from the hand of the Egyptians and to bring them out of that land into a good and spacious land, a land flowing with milk and honey the home of the Canaanites, Hittites, Amorites, Perizzites, Hivites and Jebusites. And now the cry of the people has reached me and I have seen the way the Egyptians are oppressing them. Come, I am sending you to Pharaoh to bring my people Israel out of Egypt."
> (Exod. 3:6-10)

Even after the nine plagues, the Pharaoh would not let God's people go.

The passover

Now the Lord had said to Moses:

I will bring one more plague on Pharaoh and on Egypt. After that, he will let you go from here, and when he does he will drive you out completely. Tell the people that men and women alike are to ask their neighbors for articles of silver and gold. (Exod. 11:1-3)

The Lord said to Moses and Aaron in Egypt, "This month is to be for you the first month, the first month of your year. Tell the community of Israel that on the tenth day of this month each man is to take a lamb for his family, one for each household. The animals you choose must be year old males without defect, and you may take them from the sheep or the goats. Take care of them until the fourteenth day of the month, when all the people of the community of Israel must slaughter them at twilight. Then they are to take some of the blood and put it on the sides and the tops of the doorframes of the houses, where they eat the lambs. That same night they are to eat the meat roasted over the fire, along with bitter herbs and bread made without yeast. Do not eat the meat raw or cooked in water but roast it over the fire. Do not leave any of it till the morning; if some is left till the morning, you must burn it. This is how you are to eat it: with your cloak tucked into your belt, your sandals on your feet, and your staff in your hand. Eat it in haste; it is the Lord's Passover. On that same night I will pass through Egypt and strike down every firstborn, both men and animals, and I will bring judgment on all gods of Egypt. I AM the Lord. The blood will be a sign for you on the houses where you are; and when I see the blood, I will PASSOVER you. No destructive plague will touch you when I strike Egypt." At midnight, the Lord struck down all firstborn in Egypt, from the firstborn of Pharaoh, who sat on the throne, to the firstborn of the prisoner who was in the dungeon and the firstborn of all the livestock as well.

During the night, Pharaoh summoned Moses and Aaron and said, "Up! Leave my people, you and the Israelites! Go, worship the Lord as you have requested. Take your flocks and herds, as you have said and go. And also bless me." The Israelites did as Moses instructed and asked the Egyptians for articles of silver and gold and for clothing, and they gave them what they asked for by the favor of the Lord. (Exod. 11-12)

Thus the Lord delivered his people from Egypt saved their firstborns through the blood of the lambs. Through great miracles and wonders God brought his covenant people out of slavery. But the people of Israel did not know their God. They were living in a pagan land and were more familiar with the pagan worship. So the Lord God of Israel brought them to the Sinai Desert and introduced himself to his people.

Then Moses went up to God, and the Lord called to him from the mountain and said, "This is what you are to say to the house of Jacob: You yourselves have seen what I did to Egypt, and how I carried you on eagles' wings and brought you to Myself. Now if you obey Me fully and keep my covenant, then out of all nations you will be My treasured possession. Although the whole earth is mine, you will be for Me a kingdom of priests and a holy nation." (Exod. 19:3-6)

Moses spoke these words to the people and they said we will do everything the Lord has said. Could they really do everything? Certainly not.

The law of Moses

God made a covenant with the nation of Israel at Mount Sinai. Through this covenant, God brought the whole world into the courtroom of his judgment where the character of God, his righteousness, truth, mercy, and peace were to be revealed. The law was made to be a schoolmaster to prepare Israel to receive Christ Jesus, who was to come as the savior of the world.

The purpose of the law was mainly:

To show Israel the divine standard of righteousness. (Rom. 7:12-14)
 To give a definition of sin because of man's corrupt spirit and the consciousness of sin (Rom. 3:20; 7:7; 1 John 3:4)
 To show Israel the exceeding sinfulness and deceitfulness of sin (Rom. 7:11-13; Gal. 3:19)
 To expose to all men their guilt before God (Rom. 3:19)
 To preserve Israel and the Messianic seed line from the corruption of the world. (Gal. 3:19)
 To keep Israel in the custody of the law until the coming of the Messiah (Gal. 3:22-25; 4:1-3)
 To show the two major ways of God's dealings with men, Law and Grace (John 1:17)
 To foreshadow and typify all the truths of grace and redemption in the ceremonial law, and to foreshadow the person and the work of Christ. (Rom. 2:20; Heb. 10:1; Col. 2:17)
 To provide in the ceremonial law a temporary atonement (covering) for sin so that Israel could approach God in worship and based on that God could dwell in their midst. (Heb. 9-10)
 To show *all the world* that none can be justified (made righteous) by the law, but only through grace by faith. (Rom. 3:19-22; 9:30-32; 10:1-6; Gal. 3:-16)
 To show that the Law could not give life, only Jesus Christ could give life. (Gal. 3:12, Lev. 18:5)

There were three divisions of the law:

1. The moral law (the Ten Commandments): This was the divine righteous standard of morality for human conduct in relation to God and man. (Exod. 20; 34:27, 28)

   In relationship to God as follows:
   No other gods before God
   No graven images to be made or worshipped
   No taking the name of the Lord in vain
   Keep the Sabbath Day holy to the Lord

In relation to man as follows:
Honor your father and mother
Do not murder
Do not commit adultery
Do not steal
Do not give false witness
Do not covet

2. The civil law: These laws governed every area of Israel's life: legally, socially, economically, and personally.
3. The ceremonial law: This detailed set of laws was given for the purpose of governing the sacrifices, the priest hood, the sanctuary and the festival, the atonement for sins, and the uncleanness of Israel, individually and nationally. It foreshadowed the person and work of Christ in grace and in truth.

After receiving these instructions from the Lord Moses built an altar and offered a sacrifice to God. He took the blood of the sacrificed animals and poured on the altar. Moses read the Ten Commandments and other laws to the people of Israel. Then He sprinkled the blood on the people and on the book of the covenant containing the Ten Commandments and all the laws. Then Moses said, "This blood confirms and seals the covenant the Lord has made with you in giving these laws." (Exod. 24:8)

God never intended the people of Israel to approach him by keeping the commandments. God always intended for them to approach him through a blood sacrifice for the forgiveness of sin. Pointing to Jesus Christ the Lamb of God, whom God was going to provide for the remission of the sin of the world.

Abraham's grandson whose name was Jacob, had twelve sons. God changed Jacob's name to Israel during Jacob's personal encounter with God. (Gen. 28:10-15) Israel and his sons' family went to Egypt because of a famine, and his son Joseph was in charge of the whole land of Egypt at the time. (Gen. 41:41) During the 430 years in Egypt, the people multiplied and now had become a nation which was called Israel.

They were also called the twelve tribes of Israel. The twelve tribes were Reuben, Simeon, Levi, Judah, Zebulun, Issachar, Dan, Gad, Asher, Naphthali, Joseph, and Benjamin.

Moses and his brother Aaron, the priest, were from the Levites. God chose from the tribe of Levi to minister before him as priests. The king-priesthood of Moses and Aaron prefigured the priesthood of Christ after the order of Melchizedek (Heb. 3:1, 5:1-5)

Chapter 4

The Tabernacle of Moses (Exod. 25-40)

After giving the law, God also established a Tabernacle and a priesthood and a sacrifice system as the way for the Israelites to approach God. The earthly Tabernacle was a copy of the heavenly Tabernacle.

> *God said to Moses, "Tell the people of Israel that everyone who wants to bring me an offering from this list: Gold, silver, bronze, blue cloth, purple cloth, scarlet cloth, fine-twined linen, goats hair, goat-skins, acacia wood, olive oil for the lamps, spices for the anointing oil and for the fragrant incense, onyx stones, stones to be set in the ephod, and in the breast plate. For I want the people of Israel to make me a sacred Temple where I can live among them. This home of mine shall be a tent pavilion—a Tabernacle. I will give you a drawing of the construction plan, and the details of each furniture."*
> *(Exod. 25:1-9)*

The Tabernacle is to be a place where God will meet and dwell with his covenant people. God gives Moses detailed instructions on how to build the Tabernacle (Exod. 25-27). The reason for the detailed instruction is because this earthly Tabernacle is to be patterned after the real Tabernacle in heaven (Heb. 8:5). The Tabernacle was portable so that the Israelites could carry it with them on their journey. Later on when they reached the promised land, God used King Solomon to build a permanant temple, which was glorious (1 Kings 5:8). Solomon's temple was destroyed when the Babylonians captured Jerusalem.

When the people returned to their land from captivity to Babylon they rebuilt their temple (Ezra 1:1-2). This time the temple was not so glorious due to lack of resources. King Herod later restored the temple to a grand and majestic building. In AD 70, the temple was destroyed by the Roman emperor. Only the western wall is left at the present time, also known as the Wailing Wall.

The campsite of the Tabernacle (Num. 2:2-3)

The twelve tribes of Israel camped around the Tabernacle, at specific locations as instructed by God.

Each tribe had their own tribal banner on a pole. On the eastern side was the tribe of Judah. The flag for the tribe of Judah was the lion of gold on the field of scarlet. The tribe of Ephraim was assigned to the western side and the flag was a black ox on a golden field. The tribe of Reuben was placed on the southern side and their flag was a man on the golden field. The tribe of Dan was on the northern side and the flag was with a golden eagle on a blue field. These four symbols of the flags are referred in Ezekiel and in Revelation. They are the banner of victory in Jesus Christ. Jesus Christ is revealed in the four gospels. In Mathew, he is the lion of the tribe of Judah, the King of the Jews. In Mark, he is the suffering servant, the ox. In Luke, he is the Son of Man. In John, he is the Son of God, the Supreme Being in heaven, symbolized by an eagle. As the Son of God, he represents us before God with his *own blood*.

There is only one mediator between God and men: his name is Jesus Christ.

> *For there is one God and one mediator between God and men, the Man Jesus Christ. (1 Tim. 2:5)*

He is our High Priest in the order of Melchizedek (Heb. 7:16, 17).

The Tabernacle structure was surrounded by a court. Anyone could go inside the court yard, but only the priest was allowed inside the Holy Place. And only the High Priest could enter the

Most Holy Place once a year and with the blood of a sacrificed animal. There was only one entrance to the Tabernacle, which was on the east side. There is only one way to the presence of God with blood through the gate. Revelation 5:5 says, Jesus is the Lion from the tribe of Judah. All these points to Jesus Christ who is also a descendant of King David (Matt. 1:1) who said "I Am the way, and the truth and the Life." (John 14:6) The gate points out to Jesus of Nazareth who was to come (John 10:1) "I AM the door; if anyone enters by Me, he will be saved, and will go in and out and find pasture." (John 10:9)

The Tabernacle of Moses consisted of three rooms, the outer court, the Holy Place, and the Most Holy place. In each of these rooms, God commanded certain furnishings to be placed. All had to be built according to the Divine standard, and they were built by the wisdom and the Spirit of God.

The outer court

The first article you see at the entrance was the Brazen Altar made of acacia wood and overlaid with brass. It was the only place of blood sacrifice. This was the place of blood atonement. All the sacrificial offerings were done here. The Brazen Altar is the cross of Jesus in the New Covenant. The blood of Jesus was poured out at the foot of the cross. He gave himself for us as an offering and a sacrifice to God for a sweet smelling aroma (Eph. 5:2). Why? Because all have sinned and come short of the glory of God (Rom. 3:23). The law could not save the people. Animals' blood only covered the sin of the people. It could not cleanse the guilty conscience of man which kept the people from coming to the presence of the Lord.

The wages of sin is death. (Rom. 6:23)

The life of the flesh is in the blood and without the shedding of the blood there is no forgiveness of sin. (Lev. 17:11, Heb. 9:22)

We cannot approach God with our own good deeds. The sin was the product of sinful nature in man by partaking of the tree of the good and evil. The sin nature in man must be abolished. God had a plan to do just that.

> *But Jesus, who knew no sin became sin for us that we might be the righteousness of God in Him. (2 Cor. 5:21)*

The second furniture in the outer court was the Brazen Laver, made of the looking glasses of the women of Israel. It was a place for the priest to wash their hands and feet before going into the Tabernacle to minister. It had two purposes:

1. The mirror revealed impurities
2. The water was used to cleanse the impurities.

The Lever points to our rebirth, the life of Jesus coming into us through the Spirit and the Word of God.

> *I will sprinkle clean water on you, and you will be clean; I will cleanse you from all your idols. I will give you a new heart and put a new spirit in you; I will remove from you your heart of stone and give you a heart of flesh. And I will put my Spirit in you and move you to follow my decrees and be careful to keep my laws. You will live in the land I gave your forefathers; you will be my people and I will be your God. (Ezek. 36:25-28)*

Paul says:

> *Not because of righteous works that we have done, but in agreement with His mercy, He saved us through the washing of regeneration and a renewing of the Holy Spirit, whom He has poured out richly on us through Jesus Christ our Savior, so that counted as righteous by grace, we might be made heirs in accordance with our hope of eternal life. (Titus 3:4-7)*

The Holy Place

There were three articles of furniture in the Holy Place. On the north side, there was the Table of Showbread with twelve loaves of bread placed on the table by the priest, representing the twelve tribes of Israel. On the table beside the bread, there was a vessel of wine representing the covenant meal. The bread and the wine symbolized the broken body and the shed blood of Jesus Christ in perfect commitment and obedience to the will of God, the bread and the wine being used in the New Testament Communion, remembering his death as an eternal sacrifice for all humanity.

The Golden Lamp Stand was the second article in the Holy Place on the south side of the Tabernacle. It had seven branches and seven lamps on the branches. The lamps were filled with oil and burned continually before the Lord. It was the only light in the Holy Place. The Golden Lamp Stand represents God the Father. The shaft represents Jesus Christ. The oil represents the Holy Spirit and the branches the believers in Christ who are the light bearers of God in this world. The Lamp gave light in the Holy Place. The Holy Spirit illumines the minds of the believers through the Word of God.

The next article of furniture was the Golden Altar of Incense. It was placed immediately before the curtain called "The veil," which divided the Holy Place from the Most Holy Place. Incense compounded of fragrant spices was burned on it before the Lord. Every morning and evening, the priest placed burning coals on the altar. He then sprinkles incense over the coals. When the incense touches the coals, the place was filled with a fragrant white cloud of smoke. Incense is a symbol of prayer. It represents the High Priestly prayer of Jesus Christ (John 17:9-10) and the prayers offered by the believers in Jesus Name.

The Most Holy Place

The veil separated the Holy of Holies from the Holy Place. The veil was so woven together that it cannot be torn. No one could approach the presence of God in the Old Testament except the High Priest once a year, with blood. This has been our destination ever since Adam was banished from the presence of God because of sin. Now, God himself provided the way for us to come to his presence through the blood of the Lamb of God, Jesus Christ, who is also our High Priest.

The Veil

The veil of the Tabernacle acted as a divider between the Holy Place and the Most Holy Place. It signified a separation between God and man that could only be bridged by the work of atonement. No one entered there but the High Priest on the Day of Atonement once a year. Aaron's two sons entered the veil on the day of dedication when the glory of God fell. For their sin, God judged them with death (Lev. 10:1-2).

The veil that "hid the glory" points to the glory of God that was veiled in the human body of Jesus Christ. When Jesus was crucified (the final sacrifice), God the Father split the veil of the temple from top to bottom (Matt. 27:51, Mark 15:38, Luke 23:45). It was no longer needed to hide the glory of God. The once-and-for-all perfect sacrifice was offered by Jesus Christ, the Lamb of God.

All this is from God, who reconciled us to Himself through Christ and gave us the ministry of reconciliation: that God was reconciling the world to Himself in Christ, not counting men's sin s against them. (2 Cor. 5:18, 19)

The Ark was the only piece of furniture in the Most Holy Place. This was called the Ark of the Covenant. It was the most important piece of furniture in all the Tabernacle. Acting as a lid was the Mercy Seat made of pure gold, having the figures of the Cherubim on each end of it. The contents of the Ark are three-fold: the golden pot of manna, the tablets of law, and the rod of Aaron that budded. (Heb. 9:1-5, Num. 17)

Thus the Tabernacle was God's house, God's habitation among his people. There was the very presence and glory brightness of God in visible manifestation upon the blood stained Mercy Seat. It was here that God spoke in an audible voice. The glorious presence of the Lord was evident by a cloudy and fiery pillar all through Israel's wanderings in the wilderness. The Tabernacle of the Lord, with the Ark of God's presence, traveled with Israel from the Mount of Sinai through the "wilderness wandering" to the land of promise, in the land of rest.

The Ark of the Covenant, in all its history and symbolism, was the richest of all symbols, pointing to Jesus Christ. All that the Ark was to Israel in the Old Testament, Jesus Christ is to his church. The history of the Ark is the history of Christ. As the Ark was pre-eminent in the Tabernacle and Israel, so is Christ in his church (Col. 1:17-19).

There was only *one Ark* from the Tabernacle of Moses into the Tabernacle of David and from there into the temple of Solomon the Ark journeyed!

The Ark represented the Throne of God in earth.

The Ark represented the presence of God among his people Israel.

The Ark represented the glory of God revealed in Divine order in the camp.

Tabernacle Furniture

Chapter 5

The Sacrificial Offerings (Lev. 1-7)

This system would have five types of sacrifices. Throughout the history of mankind, God painted a picture of his plan in the blood sacrifice of the innocent for the guilty and life from death. The sacrificial offerings of animals were the way God pointed to the cross of Christ. There are five types of sacrifices mentioned in the book of Leviticus. Each of these sacrifices revealed certain aspect of the final and eternal sacrifice.

There were sacrifices each morning and evening, each Sabbath Day, the first day of each month and during the special feast days of celebration. These rituals continued until God himself would come in the flash as the perfect sacrifice. This was the grace of God toward Israel through the blood of the animals their sins were covered for one year and then repeated again the following year.

The five types of offerings were as follows:

1. Sin offering
2. Trespass offering
3. Burnt offering
4. Meal offering
5. Peace offering.

The sin offering and the trespass offerings were mandatory offerings for the nation and for individual Israelites.

The sin offering: You present the sin offering to God because you are a sinner by nature which was inherited from Adam. The animal for sin offering must be spotless with no defects or blemishes. The animal foreshadows the perfect Lamb of God. You place the offering on the altar and lay your hands on the head of the animal and kill by identifying that its death is your death. Symbolically, the sins of the person are transferred to the animal. The wages of sin is death (Rom. 3:3). The priest who is ministering to the Lord then take the blood and sprinkle some on the Brazen Altar and pours the rest of it at the base of the altar. Then the priest takes the fat of the inward parts of the animal and burns it on the altar. Because this is a sin offering, the priest has to take the sacrifice away outside the camp to a place ashes are brought from the altar. The priest takes his portion, and the rest of the carcass of the animal was burned outside the camp the place of ashes, because it represented sin. Jesus Christ is our sin offering because he had never sinned and he was the perfect sacrifice without spot or blemish (1 Pet. 1:18-20). In the sin offering, the blood on the horns of the altar pointed to the blood of Jesus on the cross. All his blood was poured out at the foot of the cross. To fulfill the sin offering, Jesus went outside the city gate on a hill called Calvary to be crucified. Jesus became one with our sin nature of self-righteousness. God considered us crucified with him. We are righteous in the sight of God because we are the righteousness of God in Christ (2 Cor. 5:21). The animal sacrifices could not ever satisfy God. The book of Hebrews has explained it well.

The law is only a shadow of the good things that are coming, not the realities of themselves. For this reason it can never, by the same sacrifices repeated endlessly year after year, make perfect those who draw near to worship. If it could, would they not have stopped being offered? For the worshippers would have been cleansed once for all, and would no longer have felt guilty for their sins. But those sacrifices are an annual reminder of sins, because it is impossible for the blood of bulls and goats to take away sins. Therefore, when Christ came into the world, He said, "Sacrifice and offering you did not desire, but a body you prepared for me; with burnt offerings and sin offerings you were

not pleased. Then I said, 'Here I am—it is written about Me in the scroll—I have come to do your will, O God.'"
First He said, "Sacrifices and offerings, burnt offerings and sin offerings you did not desire, nor were you pleased with them" (although the law required them to be made) Then He said, Here I am, I have come to do your will." He sets aside the first to establish the second. And by that will, we have been made holy through the sacrifice of the body of Jesus Christ once for all. Day after day every priest stands and performs his religious duties; again and again he offers the same sacrifices which can never take away sins. But when this priest had offered for all time one sacrifice for sins, He sat down at the right hand of God. Since that time He waits for His enemies to be made His footstool, because by one sacrifice He has made perfect forever those who are being made holy. The Holy Spirit also testifies to us about this. First He says: "This is the covenant I will make with them after that time, says the Lord. I will put my laws in their hearts, and I will write them on their minds." Then He adds, "Their sins and lawless acts I will remember no more." And where these have been forgiven there is no longer any sacrifice for sin. Therefore, brothers since we have confidence to enter the Most Holy Place by the blood of Jesus by a new and living way opened for us through the curtain, that is His Body." (Heb. 10:1-20)

The trespass offering: You offer the trespass offering for the sins you have committed. As you lay hand on the animal identifying with it, you confess your particular sins. "I return in repentance and let this animal be for my atonement." The priest then sprinkles the blood on the Altar and pours out the rest at the base of the Altar. The priest gets the portion of the meat. With the offering, the individual must make restitution for any harm done to a fellow Israelite. This provides reconciliation between the persons involved.

Through the sin offering and the trespass offering, the people express the desire to be in the presence of God. (Lev. 6:2-7)

The burnt offering:

These are the regulations for the burnt offering. The burnt offering is to remain on the altar throughout the night, till

> *morning, and the fire must be kept burning on the altar. The priest shall then put on the linen clothes with linen under garments next to his body, and shall remove the ashes of the burnt offering that the fire has consumed on the altar and place them beside the altar. Then he is to take off these clothes and put on others, and carry the ashes outside the camp to a place that is ceremonially clean. The fire on the altar must be kept burning; it must not go out. Every morning the priest is to add firewood and arrange the burnt offering on the fire and burn the fat of the peace offering on it. The fire must be kept burning on the Altar continuously; it must not go out. (Lev. 1:3-17; 6:8-13)*

The burnt offering is a voluntary offering of ourselves to God. We present ourselves to God on our own free will. This is an expression of our desire to commune with God.

The Meal offering:

> *These are the regulations for the meal offering: Aaron's sons are to bring it before the Lord, in front of the altar. The priest is to take a handful of fine flour and oil, together with all the incense on the meal offering, and burn the memorial portion on the altar as an aroma pleasing to the Lord. Aaron and his sons shall eat the rest of it, but it is to be eaten without yeast in a holy place, they are to eat it in the courtyard of the Tent of meeting. It must not be baked with yeast; I have given it as their share of the offerings made to Me with fire. Like the sin offering and the Trespass offering it is most holy. Any male descendant of Aaron may eat it. It is his regular share of the offerings made to the Lord by fire for the generation to come. Whatever touches it become holy." (Lev. 2, 6:14-19)*

The meal offering symbolizes our walk in communion with God. Jesus Christ is our meal offering. (John 4:34, 8:29, 12:23-24; Luke 4:18; Eph. 5:2, 1 Pet. 2:22)

> *I tell you the truth, unless a kernel of wheat falls to the ground and dies, it remains only a single seed. But if it dies, it produces many seeds. (John 12:24)*

Through his death and resurrection, Jesus perfectly fulfilled the meal offering by becoming the bread of life. God has given us the Holy Spirit to bring us to the reality of all truth. We must submit ourselves to his guiding and enjoy the walk with God through Jesus Christ. As we fellowship with the Father, we will desire more and more to set our affection on things above and bring glory to the Father through Jesus Christ.

Peace offering:

> *The Lord said to Moses, "Say to the Israelites, 'Any one who brings a fellowship offering to the Lord is to bring part of it as a sacrifice to the Lord. With his own hand he is to bring the offering made to the Lord by fire; he is to bring the fat together with the breast, and wave the breast before the Lord as a wave offering. The priest shall burn the fat over the altar, but the breast belongs to Aaron and his sons. You are to give the right thigh of your fellowship offerings to the priest as a contribution. The son of Aaron who offers the blood and the fat of the fellowship offering shall have the right thigh as his share. From the fellowship offerings of the Israelites, I have taken the breast that is waved and the thigh that is presented and have given them to Aaron the priest and his sons as their regular share from the Israelites.'" (Lev. 7:28-34)*

The wave offering in a 'T' motion pointed to the cross of Jesus Christ. In the past, we were separated from God because of our sin. Being separated from God, we were restless and without peace. Now through the blood of Jesus Christ, we may draw near to God. We may walk in communion and fellowship with God through Jesus Christ. Jesus said, "Peace I leave with you; my peace I give you. I do not give to you as the world gives. Do not let your hearts be troubled and do not be afraid." John 14:27) Jesus has become our peace offering. Jews and Gentiles alike can come to the presence of God, who has accepted Jesus as their peace offering. From the time of Adam, this is the offering we have been looking for. Just as the Israelites had a portion of this offering for themselves, the believers have become partakers of the divine nature in the Spirit (2 Pet. 1:4).

The Priesthood:

When God gave the law to Moses, he also gave instruction to build a Tabernacle, a sacrificial system and a priesthood. The Tabernacle was a way to reveal to the people of Israel how to approach God. The Tabernacle worship centered around the sacrificial system and offerings. Each offering revealed something of the nature of the ultimate sacrifice of the Lamb of God.

God chose Aaron and his sons from the tribe of Levi to minister in the Tabernacle from generation to generation. (Exod. 28:1) No one else could function as priests in the Tabernacle. Aaron was the first High priest. At his death, he would be succeeded by his oldest son. Aaron's sons took the responsibility as priests at the age of thirty. (Num. 4:3) The High Priest was the mediator between God and the people of Israel. Aaron and his sons were anointed for their priestly office, by the sprinkling of the blood on them and their priestly garments. Their sins had to be covered with blood before they can minister before the Holy God. The most important person in the Old Testament system was the High Priest who represented Israel as a nation before God.

The Holy Garments of the High Priest

The Ephod

Because of his beautiful garment the High Priest stood out among all the people. The garments consisted of fine linen beautifully interwoven with gold, blue, purple, scarlet, and fine linen. The color combination depicts the deity, the heavenly origin, the royalty, the suffering, and the spotless righteousness of Jesus Christ. In the girdle of the Ephod and the breast place of judgment we find gold woven through, the only place gold was used in the fabric of the Tabernacle.

> *Make sacred garments for your brother Aaron,*
> *to give him dignity and honor. (Exod. 28:2)*

These are the garments they are to make: a breast piece, an ephod, a robe, a woven tunic, a turban and a sash. Have them use gold, blue, purple, and scarlet yarn and fine linen. Make the Ephod of gold, and of blue, purple scarlet yarn, and of finely twisted linen. It is to have two shoulder pieces attached to two of its corners, so it can be fastened. Take two onyx stones and engrave on them the names of the sons of Israel in the order of their birth-six names on one stone and the remaining six on the other. Engrave the names of the sons of Israel on the two stones the way a gem cutter engraves a seal. Then mount the stones in gold filigree settings and fasten them on the shoulder pieces of the ephod as memorial stones for the sons of Israel.
(Exod. 28:4-12)

Levi means *joined to* or *fastened to*. They were joined to Aaron (Num. 18:2, 4) The Levites typified the church, while Aaron was the type of Jesus Christ our High Priest. The church is joined to Jesus Christ the Spiritual Head. In his intercessory prayers, Christ always bears the names of God's children on his heart. Our union with Christ is our life and our hope. The theme of this union is very much evident in the Tabernacle studies.

The breast place of judgment

> *For the breast piece, make braided chains of pure gold, like a rope. Make two gold rings for it and fasten them to two corners of the breast piece. Fasten the two gold chains to the rings at the corners of the breast piece, and the other end of the chains to the two settings attaching them to the shoulder pieces of the ephod at the front. Also put the Urim and Thummim in the breast piece, so they may be over Aaron's heart whenever he enters the presence of The Lord." (Exod. 22-26, 30)*

Urim and Thummim are defined as lights and perfections. They are the combination of God's perfect balance, balancing perception with forbearance, justice with pardon, judgment with mercy.

> *God is light in Him there is no darkness at all. (1 John 5b)*

> *Jesus Christ is the true light that gives light to every man that was coming into the world." (John 1:9)*

Jesus Christ was the manifestation of the perfect God. For the same reason, he said:

> *He that has seen Me has seen the Father. (John 14:9)*

> *The Son is the radiance of God's glory and the exact representation of His being sustaining all things by the power of His word. (Heb. 1:3)*

Urim and Thummim were only the foreshadows of lights and perfections we have in Christ Jesus.

The robe of the ephod:

> *Make the robe of the ephod entirely of blue cloth, with an opening for the head in its center. There shall be a woven edge like a collar around this opening, so that it will not tear. Make pomegranates of blue, purple, and scarlet yarn around the hem*

> *of the robe, with gold bells between them. The gold bell and the pomegranates are alternate around the hem of the robe. Aaron must wear it when he ministers. The sound of the bells will be heard when he enters the Holy place, before the Lord and when he comes out so that he will not die. (Exod. 28:31-36)*

The full circle of golden bells and pomegranates around the hem denotes our Lord's fruitfulness on earth.

The bells were meant to be heard when the High Priest went in or came out of the Holy Place. When they hear the sound of the bells, peace comes over the people, because the sound is the evidence that the High priest is alive and will come out to meet them.

The linen coat and the linen miter

> *Weave a tunic of fine linen and make the turban of fine linen. The sash is to be the work of an embroider. (Exod. 28:39)*

These are all the Old Testament symbols of reverence before God.

The plate of pure gold

It is to attach to the turban.

> *Make a plate of pure gold and engrave on it as on a seal: HOLY TO THE LORD. Fasten a blue cord to it to be on the front of the turban (miter) It will be on Aaron's forehead, and he will bear the guilt involved in the sacred gifts the Israelites consecrate whatever their gifts may be. It will be on Aaron's forehead continually so that they will be acceptable to the Lord. (Exod. 28:36-38)*

Again God is revealing the truth about the robe of righteousness that has to come from God himself. The holy things we can do for God are tainted by our fallen nature so that our High Priest, the Lord Jesus Christ, must bear the iniquity of our righteous acts. The plate of gold on Aaron's forehead was symbolic of Christ bearing with us, even with our best intentions, gifts, and prayers. These are acceptable to God only by virtue of the shed blood of Christ. That is the reason *Christ in us* is our only hope of glory.

> *But when the king came in to see the guests, he noticed a man there who was not wearing wedding clothes. "Friend," he asked, "how did you get in here without wedding clothes?" The man was speechless.*
> *Then the king told the attendants, "Tie him hand and foot, and throw him outside, into the darkness, where there will be weeping and gnashing of teeth." (Matt. 22:11-14)*

The king had chosen the wedding garment of his choice and was given freely to the people he called. The rejection of the king's generosity was insulting to the king and we see the consequence. The High Priestly garment is a reminder of the imputed righteousness of Jesus Christ (Rom. 4:8, 22-25). Without it we cannot be admitted to the wedding supper of the Lamb. Adam's attempt of the fig leaf garment was rejected by God. Adam was clothed by God himself by the skin of an animal. So we cannot say "I am a good person, I have not done any terrible things, so I should be okay with God." Faith in the blood of the Lamb of God provided by God himself is the only righteousness we can claim.

Chapter 6

The Day of Atonement Ceremonies (Lev. 16)

The Lord commanded that Aaron not to come into the Most Holy Place at all the time but only on this one day during the year. Even then he has to carry the golden censer, with his hand full of sweet incense, bring it within the veil. As he entered within the veil, placing the incense on the fiery coals of the censer, a cloud of incense ascended, covering the Ark of glory. Without the glory cloud of incense the High Priest could not enter the Most Holy Place.

The incense represents the prayers of the mediator and intercessor.

May my prayer be set before you like incense. (Ps. 141:2)

Rising incense speaks of the ascending prayers of the saints of God. (Rev. 5:8; 8:1-5) Jesus Christ is our mediator and intercessor. He ever lives to make intercession for the saints according to the will of God. (Heb. 7:24-25)

The ceremonial washing (Lev. 16:4)

On this day, there was the special washing of water in preparation for the sacrificial offerings. Aaron washed before he entered the sanctuary and then washed again in the Holy Place after the Sanctuary had been cleaned.

The linen garments (Lev. 16:3)

On this day, Aaron laid aside the garments of glory and beauty (Exod. 28:1-5) and put on linen garments. He was fully clothed in white linen as he made the atonement. He had on linen breeches, a linen coat, a linen sash, and a linen turban. They were called "the holy garments." After making the atonement for the sanctuary and washing in the Holy Place, he was then to change back into his garment of glory and beauty.

The fine linen garments are symbolized as the Divine righteousness of Christ, and the believers are clothed with the same. (Rev. 3:4-5, 15:6, 19:7-8)

The linen garments speak of the sinless humanity of Christ while the garments of glory and beauty speak of that glory which he had with the Father before the world began. (John 17:4)

The sacrifices on the day of the atonement (reconciliation)

There were special sacrifices were offered on this day in addition to the daily sacrifices.

1. A young bullock for a sin offering (for Aaron and his house)
2. A ram for a burnt offering (for Aaron himself)
3. Two young goats for a sin offering (one goat for the Lord and the other goat for the people
4. One ram for a burnt offering for the people

All these sacrifices were pointed to the one perfect and once for all sacrifice of Jesus Christ.

The atoning ministry

The three atonements were pertained to Aaron and his household, the nation of Israel, and the sanctuary.

Only the High Priest who was consecrated and anointed to minister was to make the atonement for all other priests, for all the congregation of Israel and the sanctuary of the Lord.

Atonement for Aaron and his household

Aaron, first of all, had to bring a sin offering for himself and his own house, thus making atonement for his own household. (Lev. 16:3, 6)

After this, he presented the two goats before the Lord, casting lots as to which goat for the Lord in sacrifice and which goat will be taken in to the wilderness and released. After this, Aaron was to take the blood of the bullock for his sin offering and enter within the veil, sprinkle the blood on the Mercy Seat and seven times before the Mercy Seat. All of this was done in the midst of the rising cloud of incense from the golden censer. In this way, Aaron made atonement for his own sins and the sins of his household. (Lev. 16:5, 7-10, 11-14)

Atonement for the nation

Aaron then killed the Lord's goat for a sin offering. This was the offering for the people of Israel. He entered within the veil just as before in to the Most Holy Place and sprinkled the blood on the Mercy seat of the Ark of the Covenant and then seven times before the Mercy seat. This way he made atonement for the Nation of Israel. (Lev. 16:15)

Atonement for the sanctuary

After making atonement for himself and his household and then the nation, Aaron then made atonement for the sanctuary and its furnishings.

The scapegoat (Lev. 16:8, 10, 20-22, 26)

After Aaron had come out from the Tabernacle of the congregation, he then laid his hands on the live goat. As he did the symbolic act, he confessed over the goat all the sins, iniquities, transgressions, and uncleanness of Israel. When this was completed, the scapegoat (goat for sending away) was taken by the hand of a fit man into the wilderness. The goat was to bear away all the iniquities of the people into a land uninhabited or a land of separation. There the fit man was to release the goat into the wilderness. Upon his return to the camp he was to bathe himself in water and then take his place in the camp of the Lord and of Israel.

The goat chosen by lot for God was killed. This goat died to reconcile. Its blood was sprinkled within the veil on the Mercy seat.

This pointed to the death of Jesus, who was the Lord's goat and our sin offering. He died to reconcile us to God. His blood was brought into the heavenly Sanctuary, within the veil. Again it is explained in the book of Hebrews. (Heb. 13:11-13, 9:1-14)

The scapegoat was symbolic of Christ's ministry. The scapegoat symbolized Christ in his death to reconcile. The scapegoat symbolized Christ in his resurrection that he lives to reconcile through the believers who has been given the ministry of reconciliation (2 Cor. 5:18).

The feasts of Israel

> *Three times in the year all your men must appear before the Lord your God at the place He will choose: At the feast of unleavened Bread, The Feast of Weeks, and the feast of Tabernacles. No man should appear before the Lord empty handed: Each of you must bring a gift in proportion to the way the Lord your God has blessed you. (Deut. 16:16-17)*

In the feasts, one comes to know the fulness of the godhead, for the Father, Son, and the Holy Spirit are seen at work in these particular feasts.

There are seven feasts mentioned in Leviticus 23. Among these seven, there are three to be considered as major feasts.

The feast of Passover (Lev. 23:4-5)
The feast of Unleavened Bread (Lev. 23:6-8)
The feast of the Sheaf of First Fruits (Lev. 23:9-14)
The feast of weeks (Pentecost) (Lev. 23:15-22)
The feast of Trumpets (Lev. 23:23-25)
The feast Day of Atonement (Lev. 23:26-32)
The feast of Tabernacles (Lev. 23:33-34)

The Feast of Passover took place in the first month of Israel.
The Feast of Pentecost took place in the third month of Israel.
The Feast of Tabernacles took place in the seventh month of Israel.

The feasts and their appointments originated with the Lord. It was God's desire to meet with his people, on his terms, and his grounds of approach. They were his feasts. The Lord was the host and Israel was his guest, invited to feast with him. It was appointed to a people redeemed from slavery to Egypt and separated unto the Lord that the instructions concerning the Feasts were given and not to the Gentiles.

All the males to keep the feasts: The male or the head of the household would come to the feast, learn the ways of the Lord, and in turn take it back to his family and teach them diligently what he had learnt (Deut. 6:3-15).

None were to appear before the Lord empty: The things brought were freewill offerings, and these were according to the blessings of the Lord (Deut. 16:10-12). To appear empty-handed would be a reproach on the blessings of God or an evidence of selfishness. These freewill offerings were then distributed to the Levite, the stranger, the widow, the fatherless, or the poor and the needy.

The believers are also to minister to the poor and the needy in their freewill offerings (2 Cor. 9:7).

Promise of the preservation of inheritance: The Lord gave the nation a great promise of preservation if all the males would keep the set feasts. He promised that he would cast out enemy nations before them and enlarge their nations. He also promised that no enemy would desire their land when they went up to keep these Feasts in the set times of the year. They had assurance that in their absence the families would be looked after by the Lord (Exod. 34:24).

The place of the feasts: The people of Israel to assembled at the place where the Lord's name was recorded which was the

Sanctuary of the Lord. The purpose of building of the Tabernacle was that God might have a dwelling place in his presence and glory (Exod. 25:8).

The New Testament shows the fulfillment of God's dwelling in Christ and in his Church. The name of the Godhead bodily dwells first "in Christ" and now also in his church. The fulness of the Divine Name is the Name of the Lord Jesus Christ, the redemptive name ever to be revealed, in this world and the world to come. (Matt. 28:19; Acts 2:36; Col. 1:19, 2:9)

Jesus also said:

> *Where two or three gathered in My Name,*
> *there I am in the midst of them. (Matt. 18:20)*

The Godhead name is to be found "in Christ" and then in his church, where God has placed his name.

It is to this name that believers gather to keep the feasts of the Lord. Not in any place but in the place, where his name, his presence is recorded and the place he dwells, in the believers.

The only way one can attend the feasts of the Lord is on the basis of the blood atonement. The principle of Exodus (12:13) applies here. The blood will be a sign for you on the houses where you are; and when I see the blood, I will pass over you. No destructive plague will touch you when I strike Egypt.

And again, "For the life of the flesh is in the blood, and I have given it to you upon the altar to make an atonement for your souls: for it is the blood that makes atonement for the souls." (Lev. 17:11)

All of God's communications to the believer in festival relationship is based on the foundation of the sacrificial blood of Jesus. The blood of Jesus Christ is the perfect and only one sacrifice which God accepts during this dispensation of grace. His sacrifice is never to be repeated. All the sacrifices of the three Feasts are fulfilled in the one sacrifice of the Lord Jesus Christ at Calvary. The body and blood of Jesus, the God-Man abolished animal body and animal blood forever. When the Son of God was declared as "the Lamb of God who takes away the sin of the world," God declared from heaven "This is my beloved Son in whom I AM well pleased." (John 1:29, 36; Matt. 3:15-17)

The weekly Sabbath Days

The people of Israel worked for six days, and the seventh day was the Sabbath of rest. They were not to do any work on this day. The people were called to gather and worship the Lord near his Sanctuary. This sign was given to a people who had covenant relationship with God. Breaking the Sabbath rest was punishable by death because this day was sacred to God. (Num. 15:32-41)

The Holy Sabbath Days: These were the set feast days, which were also known as the Sabbath Days. No work has to be done on these days. These were extra Sabbath Days called the "Holy convocations." This meant that sometimes there would be two Sabbaths in the same week.

The physical days of rest pointed to the spiritual days of rest for the believers. The Sabbath rest spoke of man ceasing from his own works and entering into the works of God as shown by the works of the High Priest. We are called to cease from our own works, works of the flesh (Gal. 5:19-21) and the works of the law and find rest in Jesus Christ (Matt. 11:28-30).

Jesus Christ is our High Priest and only his work of redemption brings rest. The Christian can cease from his own works and enter into rest because of the finished work of Christ (John 17:1-3, 19:30).

The lesson here is first the sacrifice and then the rest and the feast. Without the rest you cannot feast or fellowship with the Father. Without the fellowship of the Father, there is no revelation knowledge, and without the revelation knowledge, there is no transformation from glory to glory (2 Cor. 3:18).

Chapter 7

The Prophecies Concerning the Lamb of God

The Gospel of Mathew begins with the genealogy of Jesus Christ. The record of genealogy states that Jesus Christ was the Son of David, the son of Abraham (Matt. 1:1). In the Old Testament, there are about 300 predictions, which relate to the promise of a Messiah who will come to deliver mankind.

I am only referring to some that are very relevant for the point I am trying to make.

The first mention of this promise was in Genesis 3:15. When God said to the serpent, "And I will put enmity with you and the woman, and between your offspring and hers; He will crush your head and you will strike His heal," this referred to a supernatural birth of the coming savior of the world.

The seed of woman

This phrase "seed of the woman" is not a natural order, biblically speaking. In the ancient culture, the seed is referred to always of a man or the father. All the genealogies of the Bible are traced through the fathers and not through the mother. From the Aramaic translation of the Old Testament, the Jewish people understood that the "seed of the woman" was in reference to the Messiah.

The lineage of the Promised Seed: First promise was to Abraham with whom God had covenant relation:

All people on earth will be blessed through you. (Gen. 12:3b)

The land was promised to the seed of Abraham and the throne was promised to the Greater Son of David.

As Jacob was about to die, he predicted the tribe through which the Promised Seed will come who would be a blessing to all nations.

The scepter will not depart from Judah, nor the ruler's staff from between his feet, until He comes to whom it belongs. (Gen. 49:10)

God preserved the nation of Judah through miracles over and over. God made a covenant with King David.

When your days are over and you go to be with your fathers, I will raise up your offspring to his succeed you, I will establish his kingdom. He is the one who will build a house for Me, and I will establish throne forever. I will be His Father and He will be My Son. I will never take My love away from Him as I took it away from your predecessor. I will set Him over My house and My kingdom forever; His throne will be established forever. (1 Chron. 17:11-15)

So it was predicted that the "Greater Son" of David will also be the Son of God. Jesus in his humanity came from the tribe of Judah as the Greater Son of David who had the right to the throne of David as the Son of God and his reign shall never end.

A prophet like Moses

On one occasion, Jesus spoke to the religious leaders of the time, "Do not think that I will accuse you before the Father; the one who accuses you is Moses, in whom you have set your hope. For if you believed Moses, you would believe Me; for he wrote of Me" (John 5:45-46).

Moses said in Deuteronomy 18:15, "The Lord your God will raise up for you a prophet like me from among your own brothers."

The birthplace of Jesus

The Prophet Micah records one of the most specific predictions of the Messiah. His birthplace was to be in one of the villages in the province of Judea in Palestine, in Bethlehem, the city where King David was also born.

> *But you, Bethlehem Ephrathah, though you are small among the clans of Judah, out of you will come for me one who will be ruler over Israel, whose origins are from old, from ancient times. He will stand and shepherd his flock in the strength of the Lord, in the majesty of the name of the Lord His God. And they will live securely, for then His greatness will reach to the ends of the earth. And He will be their peace. (Mic. 5:2, 4, 5)*

Though Mary and Joseph were living in Nazareth, through various circumstances God brought them to Bethlehem for the birth of Jesus, just as predicted by the prophet hundreds of years prior to Jesus's birth.

Born of a virgin

> *Therefore the Lord Himself will give you a sign: Behold, a virgin will be with child and bear a son, and she will call His Name Immanuel." (Isa. 7:14)*

> *And the angel said to her, "Do not be afraid, Mary; for you have found favor with God. And behold, you will conceive in your womb, and bear a son, and you shall name Him Jesus. He will be great, and will be called the Son of the Most High; and the Lord God will give Him the throne of His Father David; and He will reign over the house of Jacob forever; and His kingdom will have no end."*
> *And Mary said the angel, "How can this be, since I am a virgin?" And the angel answered and said to her, "The Holy Spirit will come upon you, and the power of the Most High will overshadow you; and for that reason the holy offspring shall be called the Son of God." (Luke 1:30-35)*

The song of Mary

My soul praises the Lord and my spirit rejoices in God my Savior, for He has been mindful of the humble state of his servant. From now on all generations will call me blessed, for the Mighty one has done great things for me holy is his Name. His mercy extends to those who fear him, from generation to generation. He has performed mighty deeds with his arm; he has scattered those who are proud in their inmost thoughts. He has brought down rulers from their thrones but has lifted up the humble. He has filled the hungry with good things but has sent the rich away empty. He has helped his servant Israel, remembering to be merciful to Abraham and his descendants forever, even as he said to our fathers. (Luke 1:46-55)

Isaiah predicted that a virgin would have a son and that his name would be called Emmanuel, meaning *"God is with us"* Isaiah also wrote to Israel:

For a child will be born to us, and a Son will be given to us; and the government will rest on His shoulders; and His Name will be called Wonderful, Counselor, Mighty God, Eternal Father, Prince of Peace. (Isa. 9:6)

This child is none other than the virgin-born child who is Jesus Christ.

The proclamation of the angels to the shepherds

And there were shepherds living out in the fields nearby, keeping watch over their flocks at night. And the angel of the Lord appeared to them, and the glory of the Lord shone around them, and they were terrified. But the angel said to them, "Do not be afraid. I bring you good news of great joy that will be for all the people. Today in the town of David a Savior has been born to you: you will find a baby wrapped in strips of cloth and lying in a manger." Suddenly a great company of the heavenly host appeared with the angel, praising God and saying, "Glory to

God in the highest, and on earth peace to men on whom his favor rests" So they hurried and found Mary and Joseph and the baby, who was lying in the manger. (Luke 2:8-14, 16)

The voice in the wilderness

"Behold, I am going to send My Messenger, and He will clear the way before Me. And the Lord whom you seek, suddenly come to His temple; and the messenger of the covenant, in whom you delight, behold, He is coming." says the Lord of hosts. Malchi 3:1

"A voice is calling," Clear the way for the Lord in the wilderness; make smooth in the desert a highway for our God." Isaiah 40:3

Now in those days John the Baptist came, preaching in the wilderness of Judea, saying, "Repent, for the kingdom of Heaven is at hand. For this is the one referred tto by Isaiah the prophet, saying," The voice of one crying in the wilderness, "Make ready the way of the Lord, make His paths straight!" Mathew 3:1-3

Jesus anointed by the spirit of God

Behold, My servant, whom I uphold; My chosen one in whom my soul delights. I have put My Spirit upon Him; He will bring forth justice to the nations. (Isa. 42:1)

Now it came about when all the people were baptized, that Jesus also was baptized, and while He was praying, heaven opened, and the Holy Spirit descended upon Him in bodily form like a dove, and a voice came out of heaven, "You are my Son, whom I love; with whom I Am well pleased." (Luke 3:21-22)

The next day John saw Jesus coming toward him and said," Behold, the Lamb of God, who takes away the sin of the world! This is the one I meant when I said, "A man who comes after me has surpassed me because He was before me." I myself did not know Him, but the reason I came baptizing with water was that He might be revealed to Israel.

> *Then John gave the testimony: I saw the Spirit come down from heaven as a dove and remain on Him.*
> *I would not have known him, except that the One who sent me to baptize with water told me, the man on whom you see the Spirit come down and remain is he who will baptize with the Holy Spirit.' I have seen and I testify that this is the Son of God.*
> *(John 1:29-34)*

Jesus the anointed one

About 2,700 years ago, the Prophet Isaiah gave a picture of the character of the Messiah as the Spirit of the Lord would come to rest on him.

> *And the Spirit of the Lord will rest on Him,*
> *The Spirit of wisdom and understanding,*
> *The Spirit of Councel and strength,*
> *The Spirit of knowledge and the fear of the Lord*
> *And He will delight in the fear of the Lord.*
> *And He will not judge by what His eyes see,*
> *Nor make a decision by what His ears hear;*
> *But with righteousness He will judge the poor,*
> *And decide with fairness for the afflicted of the earth;*
> *And He will strike the earth with the rod of His mouth,*
> *And with the breath of His lips He will slay the wicked.*
> *Also righteousness will be the belt about His loins,*
> *And faithfulness His belt. (Isa. 11:2-5)*

Prophecy of Isaiah concerning Jesus's miracles, signs, and wonders

> *Say to those with fearful hearts, Be strong, do not fear; your God will come, He will come with vengeance; with divine retribution He will come to save you. Then will the eyes of the blind be opened and the ears of the deaf unstopped. Then will the lame leap like a deer, and the tongue of the dumb shout for joy. Water will gush forth in the wilderness and streams in the desert. (Isa. 35:4-6)*

> *When John heard in prison what Christ was doing, he sent his disciples to ask Him, "Are you the one who was to come, or should we expect someone else?" Jesus replied, "Go back and report to John what you hear and see: The blind receive sight, the lame walk, those who have leprosy are cured, the deaf hear, the dead are raised, and the good news is preached to the poor. Blessed is the man who does not fall on account of Me." (Matt. 11:2-6)*

> *The miracles were to be the proof for the religious leaders and Israel as a nation that the "Spirit of God was upon Him "and that He was anointed to bind up the broken hearted, and set at liberty the captives of sin. (Isa. 61:1-2)*

The triumphal entry of Jesus the Messiah to Jerusalem

> *Rejoice greatly, O daughter of Zion! Shout in triumph, O daughter of Jerusalem! Behold your king is coming to you; He is just and endowed with salvation, humble, and mounted on a donkey, even on a colt,*
> *the foal of a donkey. (Zach. 9:9)*

> *And the disciples went and did just as Jesus had directed them, and brought the donkey and the colt, and laid on them their garments, on which He sat. And most of the multitude spread their garments on the road, and others were cutting branches from the trees, and spreading them in the road.*
> *And the multitudes going before Him and those followed after were crying out, saying, "Hosanna to the Son of David; blessed is He who comes in the Name of the Lord; Hosanna in the Highest." The same crowd later rejected him by crying, "Crucify Him." (Matt. 21:6-9)*

The prophecy of betrayal by a friend

> *Even my close friend in whom I trusted, who ate my bread, has lifted up his heel against me. (Ps. 41:9)*

> *I do not speak of all of you. I know the ones I have chosen; but it is that the scripture may be fulfilled, "He who eats my bread has lifted up his heel against Me." (John 13:18, 21, 26)*

> *When Jesus has said this, He was troubled in spirit, and testified, and said, "Truly, truly, I say to you, one of you will betray Me."*
> *Jesus therefore answered, "That is the one for whom I shall dip the morsel and give it to him" So when He had dipped the morsel, He took and gave it to Judas, the son of Simon Iscariot. (John 13:26)*

Jesus predicted his own death

Many occasions during his ministry, Jesus revealed to his disciples about the end of his earthly ministry and his coming death. One occasion, he said:

> *The Son of Man is to be betrayed into the hands of men, and they will kill Him, and when He has been killed, He will rise again after three days. But they did not understand this statement, and they were afraid to ask Him. (Mark 9:31, 32)*

The thirty pieces of silver

> *And I said to them, "If it is good in your sight, give me my wages; but if not, never mind!" So they weighed out thirty shekels of silver as my wages.*
> *Then the Lord said to me, "Throw it to the potter, that magnificent price at which I was valued by them." So I took the thirty shekels of silver and threw them to the potter in the house of the Lord. (Zach. 11:12, 13)*

> *Then when Judas, who had betrayed Him, saw that He had been condemned, he felt remorse and returned the thirty pieces of silver to the Chief priests and elders saying, "I have sinned by betraying innocent blood." But they said, "What is that to*

us? See to that yourself!" And he threw the pieces of silver into the Sanctuary and departed; and he went away and hanged himself. And the chief priests took the pieces of silver and said, "It is not lawful to put them into the temple treasury, since it is the price of blood." And they counseled together and with the money bought the Potter's Field as a burial place for strangers. (Matt. 27:3-7)

Here as you read the prophet Zachariah's prophecy fulfilled about five hundred years later.

Who is this the prophet talking about?

Could this be the Messiah?
The Ethiopean eunuch was reading this passage of scripture:

He was led like a sheep to the slaughter, and as a lamb before the shearer is silent, so he did not open his mouth. In his humiliation he was deprived of justice. Who can speak of his descendants? For his life was taken from the earth. (Isa. 53:7, 8)

The eunuch asked Philip the Evangelist to please tell him who is the prophet talking about? So Philip took the scroll and began with that very passage and told him the good news about Jesus. And the eunuch believed the message and was baptized. (Acts 8:30-35)

The suffering and the glory of the servant

Behold My Servant shall deal wisely and shall prosper; He shall be exalted and extolled and shall stand very high. For many the servant of God became an object of horror; many were astonished at Him. His face and His whole appearance were marred more than any man's, and His form beyond that of the sons of men-but just as many were astonished at Him. So shall He startle and sprinkle many nations, and kings shall shut their mouths because of Him; for that which has been told them shall they see, and that which they have not heard shall they consider and understand. (Isa. 52:13-15) (Amplified Bible version)

Man's view of the servant: despised and rejected

Who has believed what we have heard? And to whom has the arm of the Lord been disclosed? For the Servant of God grew up before Him like a tender plant, like a root out of dry ground; He has no form or comeliness (royal, kingly pomp) that we should look at Him, and no beauty that we should desire Him, He was despised and rejected and forsaken by men, a Man of sorrows and pains, and acquainted with grief and sickness; and like One from Whom men hide their faces He was despised, and we did not appreciate His worth or have any esteem for Him. (Isa. 53:1, 2, 3)

God's view of the servant: the redeemer

Surely He has born our griefs (sickness, weakness and distress) and carried our sorrows and pains (of punishment), yet we (ignorantly) considered Him stricken, smitten, and afflicted by God (as if with leprosy)
But He was wounded for our transgressions, He was bruised for for our guilt and iniquities; upon Him was the chastisement that made us whole, and with the stripes (that wounded) Him we are healed and made whole. All we like sheep have gone astray, we have turned every one to his own way; and the Lord has laid on Him the guilt and the iniquity of us all. (Isa. 53; 4-6)

Man's view of his death as failure

He was oppressed, (yet when) He was afflicted, He was submissive and opened not His mouth; like lamb that is led to the slaughter, and as a sheep before her shearers is dumb, so He opened not His mouth. By oppression and judgment He was taken away.; and as for His generation who among them considered that He was cut out of the land of living (stricken to His death) for the transgression of my (Isaiah's) people, to whom the stroke was due? And they assigned Him a grave with the wicked, and with a rich man in His death, although He had done no violence, neither was any deceit in His mouth. (Isa. 53:7-9)

God's view of the servant's death as victorious

Yet it was the will of the Lord to bruise Him; he has put him to grief; when He makes His life an offering for sin. He shall see His (spiritual) offspring, He shall prolong His days, and the will and pleasure of the Lord shall prosper in His hand. He shall see the fruit of the travail of His soul and be satisfied; by His knowledge of Himself (which He possesses and imparts to others) shall My (uncompromisingly) righteous One, My Servant, justify many and make many righteous (upright and in right standing with God) for He shall bear their iniquities and their guilt (with the consequences, says the Lord). Therefore will I divide Him a portion with the great (kings and rulers) and He shall divide the spoil with the mighty, because He poured out His Life unto death, and (He let Himself) be regarded as a criminal and be numbered with the transgressors; yet He bore (and took away) the sin of many and made intercession for the transgressors. (Isa. 53:10-12)

He opened not his mouth (Isa. 53:7)

And while He was being accused by the chief priests and elders, He made no answer. Then Pilate said to Him, "Do you not hear how many things they testify against You?" And He did not answer him with regard to a single charge, so that the governor was quite amazed. (Matt. 27:12-14)

When the officers came to seize Jesus to arrest him, he willingly came out to them. When Peter tried to defend him, Jesus tried to stop him by saying, "All this has taken place that the scripture of the prophets may be fulfilled" (Matt. 26:56).

By his stripes we are healed (Isa. 53:5)

"But He was wounded for our transgressions, He was bruised for our iniquities; the chastisement of our peace was upon Him, and by His stripes we are healed."

Then Pilate took Jesus and had Him flogged. The soldiers twisted together a crown of horns and put it on His head. They clothed Him in a purple robe and went up to Him again and again saying,' Hail, O king of the Jews!" and they struck Him in the face. (John 19:1-3)

The suffering of the servant foretold by King David

My God, My God, why have you forsaken Me? But I Am a worm and not a man, scorned by men and despised by the people. All who see Me mock Me; they hurl insults, shaking their heads: "He trusts in the Lord; let the Lord rescue Him, since He delights in Him." I Am poured out like water and all My bones are out of joint. My heart has turned to wax; it has melted away within Me. My strength is dried up like a potsherd, and My tongue sticks to the roof of My mouth; you lay Me in the dust of death. Dogs have surrounded Me; a band of evil men has encircled Me, they have pierced My hands and My feet. I can count all My bones; people stare and gloat over Me. They divide My garments among them and cast lots for My clothing. (Psa. 22:1, 6-8, 14-18)

When the soldiers crucified Jesus, they took His clothes, dividing into four shares, one for each of them, with the undergarment remaining. This garment was seamless, woven in one piece from top to bottom. "Let us not tear it," they said to one another. "Let us decide by lot who will get it." This happened that the Scripture might be fulfilled which said, "They divided My garments among them and cast lots for my clothing." So this is what the soldiers did. (John 19:23-24)

A jar of wine vinegar was there, so they soaked a sponge in it, put sponge on a stalk of the hyssop plant, and lifted it to Jesus' lips. (John 19:29) (See also Ps. 69:21, 22:15)

Sins of the world cuts of Jesus from the presence of the

Father

And about the ninth hour Jesus cried out with a loud voice, saying, "Eli, Eli, lama sabachthani?" that is "My God, My God, Why have you forsaken Me?" (Ps. 22:1; Matt. 27:46)

Nature responds in violence at the time of crucifixion

I will show wonders in heaves and on the earth, blood and fire and billows of smoke. The sun will be turned to darkness and the moon to blood before the coming of the great and dreadful day of the Lord. (Joel 2:30-31)

"From the sixth hour until the ninth hour darkness came over all the land And when Jesus had cried out in a loud voice, He gave up His Spirit. At that moment the curtain of the Temple was torn in two from top to bottom. The earth shook and the rocks split. The tombs broke open and the bodies of many holy people who had died were raise to life. They came out of the tombs, and after Jesus' resurrection they went into the holy city and appeared to many people." (Matt. 27:45, 50, 51)

Not a bone broken.

They shall leave none of it until morning, nor break a bone of it; according to all the regulations of the Passover they shall observe it. (Num. 9:12)

The soldiers therefore came and broke the legs of the first man who had been crucified with Jesus, then those of the other. But when they came to Jesus and found that He was already dead, they did not break His legs. (John 19:32, 33)

He was pierced

"And I will pour out on the house of David and on the inhabitants of Jerusalem the Spirit of grace and supplication, so that they will look on Me whom they have pierced; and they will mourn for Him, as one mourns for an only son, and they

*weep bitterly over Him, like the bitter weeping over a firstborn."
(Zach. 12:10)*

Instead one of the soldiers pierced Jesus' side with a spear, bringing a sudden flow of blood and water. The man who saw it has given testimony, and his testimony is true. He knows that he tells the truth, and he testifies so that you also believe. These things happened so that the Scripture would be fulfilled. "Not one of His bones will be broken" and as another Scripture says, "They will look on the one they have pierced." (John 19:34-37)

The Lamb of God who came to take away the sin of the world

"Sacrifice and offering you did not desire, but a body you have prepared for Me, burnt offerings and sin offerings you did not require. Then I said, "Here I AM, I have come-it is written about Me in the scroll. To do your will, O My God is My desire; your law is within My heart." (Psa. 40:6-8)

God had no pleasure in the Old Testament sacrificial system even though it was his divinely ordained way of dealing with sin at the time. But God prepared a body for the Promised One, who was to come and do God's will on this earth. As we have seen through the Old Testament prophecies, Jesus Christ has fulfilled every prophecy concerning the Lamb of God, who became the ultimate sacrifice once for all. Therefore, sacrifices are no longer needed.

And by that will, we have been made holy through the sacrifice of the body of Jesus Christ once for all. Day after day every priest stands and performs his religious duties; again and again he offers the same sacrifices, which can never take away sins. But when this Priest had offered for all time one sacrifice for sins, He sat down at the right hand of God. Since that time He waits for His enemies to be made His footstool, because by one sacrifice He has made perfect forever those who are being made holy. (Heb. 10:10-14)

The burial of Jesus

His grave was assigned to be with wicked men, yet with a rich man in His death; although He had done no violence, nor was there any deceit in His mouth. (Isa. 53:9)

"As evening approached, there came a rich man from Arimathea, named Joseph, who had himself become a disciple of Jesus. Going to Pilate, he asked for Jesus' body, and Pilate ordered that it be given to him. Joseph took the body, and wrapped it in a clean cloth, and placed it in his own new tomb that he had cut out of the rock. He rolled a big stone in front of the entrance to the tomb and went away." (Matt. 27:57-60)

Joseph of Arimathea, without realizing, fulfilled Isaiah's prophecy, some seven hundred years before Jesus's death.

The resurrection of Jesus

I saw the Lord always before me. Because he is at my right hand, I will not be shaken. Therefore my heart is glad and my tongue rejoices; my body also will rest secure, because you will not abandon me to the grave, nor will you let your Holy one see decay. You have made known to me the paths of life; you will fill me with joy in your presence. (Psa. 16:8-11, NIV)

Peter's message on the Day of Pentecost

Men of Israel, listen to this: Jesus of Nazareth was a man accredited by God to you by miracles, wonders and signs, which God did among you through Him, as you yourself know. This Man was handed over to you by God's set purpose and foreknowledge; and you, with the help of wicked men, put Him to death by nailing Him to the cross. But God raised Him from the dead, freeing Him from the agony of death, because it was impossible for death to keep its hold on Him. David said about Him: "I saw the Lord always before me. Because he is at my right hand, I will not be shaken. Therefore my heart is glad and my tongue rejoices; my body also will live in hope, because You will not abandon me to the grave, nor will you let your Holy One see decay. You have made known to me the paths of life; you will fill me with joy in your presence." (Ps. 16:8-11; Acts 2:22-34, 36)

Brothers, I can tell you confidently that the patriarch David died and was buried, and his tomb is here to this day. But he was a prophet and knew that God had promised him on oath that He would place one of his descendants on his throne. Seeing what was ahead, he spoke of the resurrection of the Christ, that he was not abandoned to the grave, nor His body see decay. God has raised this Jesus to life, and we are all witnesses of the fact. Exalted to the right hand of God, He has received from the Father the promised Holy Spirit and has poured out what you now see and hear. For David did not ascend to heaven, and yet he said, "The Lord said to my Lord: 'Sit at my right hand until I make your enemies a footstool for your feet' (Ps. 110:1). Therefore let all Israel be assured of this: God has made this Jesus, whom you crucified, both Lord and Christ."

The ascension of Jesus Christ

The Lord says to my Lord: "Sit at my right hand until I make your enemies a footstool for your feet The Lord will extend your mighty scepter from Zion; rule in the midst of your enemies." (Ps. 110:1-2)

Then Jesus came to them and said, "All authority in heaven and on earth has been given to Me."

After He said this He was taken up before their eyes, and a cloud hid Him from their sight. They were looking intently up in to the sky as He was going, when suddenly two men dressed in white stood beside them. Men of Galilee," they said, "why do you stand here looking into the sky? This same Jesus, who has been taken from you into heaven, will come back in the same way you have seen Him go into heaven. (Matt. 28:18, Acts 1:9)

Chapter 8

The New Covenant

The New Covenant was made by the Lord Jesus Christ prior to his death at Jerusalem. It was made with the twelve apostles, who represented the House of Israel and the House of Judah after the flesh. They became the pillar of the church being the apostles of the Lamb.

The New Covenant prophesied: God was not satisfied with the Old Covenant and the animal sacrifices. He foretold that one day in the future he will make a New Covenant with the House of Israel.

> "The redeemer will come to Zion, to those in Jacob who repent of their sins," declares the Lord.
> "As for me, this is My covenant with them," says the Lord. "My Spirit, who is on you, and my words I have put in your mouth will not depart from your mouth, or from the mouths of their descendants from this time on and forever." (Isa. 59:20, 21)

> "The time is coming," declares the Lord, "when I will make a New Covenant with the House of Israel and with the House of Judah. It will not be like the covenant I made with their forefathers when I took them by the hand to lead them out of Egypt, because they broke my covenant, though I was a husband to them. This is the covenant I will make with the house of Israel after that time."

"I will put my law in their minds and write it on their hearts. I will be their God, and they will be my people. No longer will a man teach his neighbor, or a man his brother, saying, 'Know the Lord,' because they will all know me, from the least of them to the greatest," declares the Lord. "For I will forgive their wickedness and remember their sins no more." (Jer. 31:31-34)

The Prophet Jeremiah gave a clear and full prophecy concerning the New Covenant that the Lord said He would make with the house of Israel and the House of Judah in the last days. The writer of Hebrews also referred to this in the book of Hebrews, Chapter 8. The promises of the New Covenant involved a new heart and a new mind upon which the laws of God would be written instead of upon the tablets of stone.

I will make a covenant of peace with them and rid the land of wild beasts so that they may live in the desert and sleep in the forests in safety. I will bless them and the places surrounding my hill. I will send down showers in season; there will be showers of blessing. (Eze. 34:25, 26)

These prophets of Israel were under the Old Covenant they prophesied of the New Covenant, which would be better.

After the three and a half years of ministry on the tenth day of the month of Passover the "Lamb of God" entered Jerusalem. He was received with cheers and praises by the people saying, "Blessed is He who comes in the Name of the Lord" (John 12:13). For five days the religious leaders examined him. He was found to be spotless and without blemish. He was born to die as the Passover Lamb.

The Passover meal

The Lord Jesus Christ prior to his crucifixion, established an ordinance by which the believers could remember him and partake of his table or the Communion (Matt. 26:26-28; Luke 22:19, 20). The bread broken symbolized his broken body. The wine symbolized his outpoured blood. Paul received special revelation about the Communion table and wrote to the

Corinthian church concerning the need of eating and drinking worthily of the body and blood of Christ (1 Cor. 11:23-24). Each time believers gather together at the communion, we are proclaiming the finished work of Jesus at the cross, our union and fellowship with him and with each other. We are celebrating the life given for us and the life we have received from him. We need only to offer spiritual sacrifices as believers, such as offering of our bodies as a living sacrifice (Rom. 12:1, 2) and sacrifice of praises (Heb. 13:15) and sacrifice of fellowship (Heb. 12:16).

The Holy Body and the Holy Blood of Jesus

The Body: The book of Hebrews, Chapter 9 deals with the body and Chapter 10 deals with the blood showing the supremacy of Jesus' body and blood over animal body and blood. The body and blood of Jesus did not perish at the cross, nor did they see corruption. They are in heaven for us and have been accepted by the Father as the basis of Christ's intercessory ministry. Christ's body in heaven will be the eternal evidence of his perfect sacrifice. His body now glorified still has the wounds in his hands feet and side where they pierced (John 20:24). Christ's body in heaven is the guarantee that the bodies of the believers in Christ will be raised and glorified (Phil. 3:20-21). The one sacrifice of Jesus's body forever fulfills and abolishes all previous sacrifices. His sacrifice as a Lamb of God will remain eternally before the throne of God. The cross was the altar on which Jesus Christ was sacrificed by the Father.

The Blood: The blood of Christ is the most precious thing in the universe. It is the only thing that can cleanse our conscience of sin (John 1:29, 36; Rev. 5:6; Heb. 13:10-13).

> *It is also the blood of God, the divine life that speaks for us.*
> *(1 Pet. 1:8-20)*

> *All true believers have faith in the precious blood of Jesus that was shed on Calvary's cross. (Heb. 12:22-24)*

The benefits from the blood of Jesus

Cleansing from sin by the blood (1 John 1:7)
Justification by the blood (Rom. 5:9)
Redemption through the blood (Eph. 1:7)
Reconciliation through the blood (Rom. 3:25)
Peace with God through the blood (Col. 1:20)
Approach God by the blood (Eph. 2:13)
Conscience purged through the blood (Heb. 9:13)
Sanctification by the blood (Heb. 13:12)
Overcome Satan by the blood (Rev. 12:11)
Eternal life through the blood (John 6:53-63)

The atoning work of Jesus Christ, the Lamb of God

An atonement (Rom. 5:11, John 1:29, 36)
A propitiation (1 John 2:2, 4:10; Rom. 3:25)
A substitution (Rom. 5:8; 1 Pet. 3:18)
A redemption (Col. 1:14)
A ransom (1 Tim. 2:5, 6)
A reconciliation (2 Cor. 5:18-21; Heb. 2:17)

Christ took our sins and iniquities and suffered the wrath of a Holy God, receiving the penalty which was death. Christ fulfilled all the Old Testament requirements of the law, the Psalms, and the prophets.

The benefits of the salvation

Salvation means, safety, security, preservation, deliverance, and wholeness.

The greatest blessing of salvation is the spiritual blessings in Christ. (Eph. 1:3)

The forgiveness and remission of the penalty of sin. (Acts 10:43, 13:36-39)

Justification: A declaration of righteousness before God through Christ (Rom. 5:1). The New Covenant make it possible for justification by faith in the finished work of Christ (Rom. 3:19, 20).

Regeneration: Under the Old Covenant none could be born into the family of God, in the New Covenant through regeneration the believer is born into the family of God and call God "Father" (John 3:1-5).

Sanctification: The process of adoption by the Father. The Holy Spirit is given to us to be a custodian to teach and train us to live in the house of God.

Adoption: Jesus Christ is the First born among the Family of brethren (Rom. 8:29). We are also placed as sons in the family of God (Rom. 8:15, 23; Gal. 4:5).

Glorification: It is the final work of redemption of the believers. The New Covenant makes provision for the believer from justification to glorification (Rom. 8:17, 30). The Old Covenant people experienced the brightness and glory of God from distance, whereas the New Covenant brings the believer into the fulness of the glory of God (John 17:22-24; 2 Cor. 3:18).

The Lamb of God is on the throne

The blood of the Lamb destroyed the serpent and set us free from bondage to him. Believers are covered with the blood of Jesus and sealed by the Holy Spirit. Death is swallowed up in victory. God has given us the victory through Jesus Christ our Lord (1 Cor. 15:54-58).

That power is like the working of His mighty strength, which He exerted in Christ when He raised Him from the dead and seated Him at his right hand in the heavenly realms, far above all rule and authority, power and dominion and every title that can be given, not only in this world, but also in the world to come. And God placed all things under His feet and appointed Him to be Head over everything for the church, which is His body, the fullness of Him who fills everything in every way. (Eph. 1:19-23)

The seed of the woman has bruised the head of the serpent just as God said in Genesis 3:15.

All you have to do is come and receive the gift of salvation. It is free for whoever comes to God through Jesus Christ that you might have fellowship with God and be in his presence forever.

In the Book of Revelation, it is written that John saw the Lamb on the throne.

Then I saw in the right of him who sat on the Throne a scroll with writing on both sides and sealed with seven seals. And I saw a mighty angel proclaiming in a loud voice, "Who is worthy to break the seals and open the scroll?" But no one in heaven or on earth or under the earth could open the scroll or even look inside it. Then one of the elders said to me, "Do not weep! See the lion of the tribe of Judah, the Root of David, has triumphed. He is able to open the scroll and its seven seals." (Rev. 5:1-3, 5)

Then John saw the Lamb, who took the scroll from the one who was sitting on the throne, the elders fell down before the Lamb, and they sang a new song.

Chapter 9

Reconciliation

And God was reconciling the world to Himself in Christ, not counting men's sins against them. (2 Cor. 5:19a)

Reconciliation applies to the soul. It is the soul of Adam that sinned first; it is the soul that must be reconciled first. We need to be reconciled because there was a chasm between God and man. All were dead in trespasses and sin due to the inherent Satan nature in man. It is the Satan nature that blinded human beings and they became rebellious and enemies of God. A bridge had to be built between God and man. God gave his Son Jesus the cup to drink, the cup of all the satanic poison in the world along with everything that works death in the world. Jesus was not born with the sin nature of Adam like every other man. While Jesus had an earthly mother; the seed and his nature came from the Father through the Holy Spirit overshadowing the Virgin Mary (Luke 1:35). Jesus knew that on one Passover, he would become the eternal Passover Lamb to take away the sins of the world.

God made Him who knew no sin to be sin for us, that we might become the righteousness of God in Him. (2 Cor. 5:21)

Jesus said in John 3:14 that "Just as Moses lifted up the snake in the desert, so the Son of Man must be lifted up" (Num. 21:9). But if I, when I am lifted up from the earth, will draw all men to myself" (John 12:32). The death of Jesus on the cross made reconciliation possible. The one thing that kept human being from knowing God was the Satan nature. Now that is taken care of, the Father is drawing all men to Jesus Christ. "But we see Jesus, who was made a little lower than angels, now crowned with glory and honor because He suffered death, so that by the grace of God He might taste death for every one (Heb. 2:9).

Reconciliation by the cross makes it possible for the Holy Spirit to work in the soul-mind of those who have not been born again, giving once again the power of choice. The second chance for people to choose the Tree of Life (Jesus) This choice was lost to us because Adam chose for all of us. The sacrifice of God's Lamb ended the enmity. Christ carried all our sin to the cross and God does not hold it against us any more.

For if, when we were enemies, we were reconciled to God by the death of his Son, much more, being reconciled, we shall be saved by His life. (Rom. 5:10)

This scripture has two important truths in it which are as follows:

1. We are reconciled by his death two thousand years ago on the cross when Jesus died.
2. We shall be saved by His life.

There are three levels of understanding about what happened at the cross. They are as follows:

The first level: It is the death of our old man, which is the soul level, and reconciliation by the death of the Son of God and forgiveness of sin.

That God was reconciling the world to himself in Christ, not counting men's sins against them. (2 Cor. 5:19a)

The scripture is clear; now that the sins are forgiven, the opportunity is set before everyone to become a child of God. In the Old Testament time, through the atonement, everyone received pardon for their sins, but they could not become the children of God. Likewise, Christ brought forgiveness of sin to the whole world. Now, the Lord is waiting for each of us to accept his finished work on Calvary's cross. Therefore, all we have to do is believe on the Lord Jesus and you will be saved (Acts 16:31).

The second level: It is the time, when Christ spent three days and three nights in the belly of the earth.

For as Jonah was three days and three nights in the belly of a huge fish, so the Son of Man will be three days and three nights in the heart of the earth. (Matt. 12:40)

This is where Christ had the final victory over Satan. Jesus took the keys of death, hell, and grave.

O death, where is thy sting? O grave, where is thy victory? The sting of death is sin; and the strength of sin is the law. (1 Cor. 15:55-56)

The sting of death and hell are swallowed up in victory. Our personal sins were never a problem. It was the original sin that caused us to sin.

The third level: It deals with the exchange of natures. We are saved by His life, having the life of Christ within us and being filled with His divine nature. This is our personal Passover. Our new birth is the release from the bondage and slavery of Satan.

The spiritual birth

This has to do with the spirit part of man with the nature of Satan. During the discourse with Nicodemus, in John 3:1-8, Jesus said, "I will tell you the truth, unless a man is born again he cannot see the kingdom of God." There was no other mention of it in the gospels. There is one other scripture in 1 Peter 1:23 which uses the word *born again*. However, there are more than two hundred scriptures referring to "in Christ, Christ in you and in God." The finished work of Jesus on the cross is what makes it possible. Simply believing on the work of the cross and believing that Jesus carried your sin away, you will receive salvation.

> *That if you confess with your mouth, "Jesus is Lord," and believe in your heart that God raised Him from the dead, you will be saved. For it is with your heart that you believe and are justified, and it is with your mouth that you confess and are saved. As the scripture says, "Every one who trust in Him will never be put to shame." For there is no difference between Jew and Gentile, the same Lord is Lord of all and richly blesses all who call on Him, for everyone who calls on the Name of the Lord will be saved. (Rom. 10:9-13)*

God originated and directed and completed all things concerning our salvation.

> *For by grace you are saved through faith: and that not of yourselves: it is the gift of God: Not of works, lest any man should boast. (Eph. 2:8-9)*

Jesus said that the Holy Spirit would be sent to convict the world of the sin of unbelief, and of the righteousness of Christ, and of judgment of Satan (John 16:7-11). The Holy Spirit calls and sends messengers to preach the true gospel of the Lord Jesus Christ based on grace by his finished work on the cross, because preaching of the cross is the power of God unto salvation to everyone who believes (1 Cor. 1:18; Rom. 1:16). The Holy Spirit then takes and applies the Word preached to the heart of man and builds a foundation of faith.

> *"Faith comes by hearing and hearing by the word of Christ." (Rom. 10:17)*

The moment we believe, the Holy Spirit baptizes us into the body of Christ (1 Cor. 12:13). We are literally born again by the Spirit of Christ, the incorruptible Word, the eternal seed, and nature of the Father being implanted in us (1 Pet. 1:23; 2 Pet. 1:4). The very life of Christ is in the believer. Believers have eternal life and the divine nature in us, the satanic nature was completely removed from us by the Life of Christ in us. We have been fully born again by the grace of God and not that of ourselves. God's love desired us; his mercy and grace bought us and redeemed us.

His Spirit called and birthed us. We are now the new creation beings that never existed before (2 Cor. 5:17). We have no ties to the old Adam's race. The Father sees the Son in us and he is well pleased. We have this treasure in our earthen vessel. We are the living, walking, and talking Tabernacle of God on this earth. Christ has returned and living in his body the church. This is the mystery that was hidden through the ages and now revealed to us by his Holy Spirit (1 Cor. 2:7-10). We cannot know these things through our five senses but by revelation through the Spirit of God (1 Cor. 2:9). As the new creation beings, we are not in covenant with God because we are birthed sons of God. We were chosen in Christ from before the foundation of the world (Eph. 1:4). We have no past. Our past is in Christ, our present is in Christ, and our future is in Christ. We are blessed with all spiritual blessings in heavenly places in Christ Jesus (Eph. 1:3). For the believers, all promises are yes and Amen in Christ Jesus! (2 Cor. 1:20)

The revelation

The church of Jesus Christ is built on the rock of revelation. The heart of revelation cannot be understood by the natural mind or senses (1 Cor. 2:9). Jesus asked Peter:

> *Who do you say I am?"* Simon Peter answered, *"You are the Christ, the Son of the living God."* Jesus replied, *"Blessed are you Simon son of Jonah, for this was not revealed to you by man, but by my Father in heaven." (Matt. 16:15a, 16, 17)*

The church is being built on the rock of revelation knowledge, the knowledge that existed before the fall of Adam. Men everywhere operates through the knowledge of good and evil that comes through the natural mind. But the born-again child of God has access to the knowledge through revelation by the Spirit of God. It is this revelation knowledge that Christ told Peter would keep the gates of hell from locking the church out of what it is doing in this earth (Matt. 16:18).

The revelation knowledge that God chose us in Christ before the foundation of the world (Eph. 1:4).

The Lamb was slain before the foundation of the world (Rev. 13:8). The eternal plan of God was consummated by Jesus Christ (1 Pet. 1:20). Christ is the living revelation. Christ now lives his resurrection life in and through us. Christ's Spirit birthed in us is our eternal life source. It is through Christ in us that we fellowship with the Father.

> *None of the rulers of this age understood it, for if they had, they would not have crucified the Lord of glory. However as it is written: "No eye has seen, no ear has heard, no mind has conceived, what God has prepared for those who love Him," but God has revealed it to us by His Spirit. The Spirit searches all things, even the deep things of God. For who among men knows the thought of a man except the man's spirit within him? In the same way no one knows the thoughts of God except the Spirit of God. We have not received, the spirit of the world but the Spirit who is from God, that we may understand what God has freely given us. (1 Cor. 2:8-12)*

The ministry of the Holy Spirit

Jesus lived by the life of the Father in him. Jesus taught by the life of the Father in him. The disciples were taught all things by Jesus, the Son of God through the Person of the Father, who lived in him. The disciples were taught in truth by the voice of the Father through Jesus. Jesus told them that it was necessary and to their advantage that he go away to the Father (John 16:7).

> *And I will ask the Father, and he will give you another Counselor to be with you forever-the Spirit of Truth. But the Counselor, the Holy Spirit, whom the Father will send in my name, will teach you all things and remind you of everything I have said to you. But when He the Spirit of truth, comes, he will guide you into all truth. He will bring glory to me by taking from what is mine and making it known to you.*
> *(John 14:16, 26, 15:13, 14)*

The Holy Spirit was sent as promised on the day of Pentecost to begin the church. The Holy Spirit is "the Spirit of truth" who rightly divides the "word of truth" (2 Tim. 2:15). The Holy Spirit is the true teacher of all. Those who are gifted to teach in the body of Christ are facilitators to point men to the Holy Spirit and to confirm what the Holy Spirit is teaching. The Father wants to fellowship with us as sons. The Holy Spirit renews our mind until we understand that Christ lives in us to be our only life. The Holy Spirit is not Christ. Christ has come to live in the believer as the believers life (Gal. 2:20).

> *He who has the Son in him has life, and he who does not have the Son of God has no life. (1 John 5:12)*

> *The Holy Spirit works in our soul-mind. We are to be taught by the anointing within us. (1 John 2:27)*

> *As Christ is revealed in us by the Holy Spirit, the Spirit of His Son in us will cry out "Abba, Father." (Gal. 4:6; Rom. 8:15)*

> *For those who are led by the Spirit of God are called the sons of God. (Rom. 8:14)*

Chapter 10

The Gospel of Grace

While it is true that all scripture is God-breathed and is useful for teaching, rebuking, correcting, and training in righteousness so that the man of God may be thoroughly equipped for every good work (2 Tim. 3:16). Some of the scriptures are written for certain specific people in mind at the time it was written. These specific scriptures have practical application for everyone.

The traditional Gospel of Jesus of Nazareth (Christ in the flesh) was preached to the nation of Israel. God made all the Old Covenants with Israel and was promised to them that he would make a New Covenant with them in his time. Jesus made the New Covenant with the house of Israel and Judah represented by the twelve apostles.

> *These twelve, Jesus sent out with the following instructions: Do not go among the Gentiles or enter any towns of the Samaritans, Go rather to the lost sheep of Israel. As you go preach this message: "The kingdom of heaven is near." (Matt. 10:5-7)*

This gospel was focused on restoring the kingdom on earth for the Jewish people Jesus as their Messiah King. It was given to the people who will remain on earth. This was preached to them before the crucifixion of Jesus Christ. The gospel was still under the law and was given to Israel the law people who were not Spirit birthed sons of God. Commingling, these two messages cause a lot of confusion in the church. The account written by Apostle John is different because John refers to the union of the believer with Jesus Christ which is for the new creation race of people born from above, whose father is God.

Paul's conversion

As he neared Damascus on his journey, suddenly a light from heaven flashed around him. He fell to the ground and heard a voice say to him, "Saul, Saul why do you persecute Me?" "Who are you Lord?" Saul asked. "I Am Jesus, whom you are persecuting." He replied. "Now get up and go into the city and you will be told what you must do." (Acts 9:3-6)

Paul, who was also known as Saul, was persecuting all those who followed Jesus Christ in those days. He was on the way to Damascus to find Christian men and women and bring them to Jerusalem as prisoners, when he had the encounter with the Lord Jesus Christ. He was blind for three days, and a man by the name of Ananias prayed for him, and Paul received his sight and was spirit birthed at the same time. Paul's own account of his salvation is written in the book of Acts 22:3-16.

Paul receives revelation from Jesus Christ

Paul a servant of Christ Jesus, called to be an apostle and set apart for the gospel of God-the gospel he promised beforehand through his prophets in the holy scriptures regarding His Son, who as to His human nature was a descendant of David, and who through the Spirit of holiness was declared with power to be the Son of God by His resurrection from the dead: Jesus Christ our Lord. Through Him and for His Name sake, we received grace and apostleship to call people from among all the Gentiles to the obedience that comes from faith. (Rom. 1:1-5)

But when God, who set me apart from birth and called me by His grace, was pleased to reveal His Son in me. So that I might preach Him among the Gentiles, I did not consult any man, nor did I go up to Jerusalem to see those who were apostles before I was, but I went immediately in to Arabia and later returned to Damascus. (Gal. 1:15-17)

I want you to know brothers, that the gospel I preached is not something man made up, I did not receive it from any man, nor was I taught it; rather, I received it by revelation from Jesus Christ. (Gal. 1:11-12)

Paul received the revelation that Christ lives in the born again believer, let us not confuse this with the Holy Spirit who came into us and works in the mind to transform it. Christ lives in us and He alone is our life.

I have been crucified with Christ and I no longer live, but Christ lives in me. (Gal. 2:20a)

We are Spirit birthed children of God in Christ Jesus. We are also a heavenly people, seated in heavenly places in Christ Jesus.

For you died, and your life is now hidden with Christ in God. When Christ, who is your life, appears, then you also will appear with Him in glory. (Col. 3:3-4)

There are about 200 scriptures referring to our in Christ position in Paul's epistles.

Paul speaks about his gospel at least in three places in his letters to the church.

This will take place on the day when God will judge men's secrets through Jesus Christ, as my gospel declares. (Rom. 2:16)

Now to Him who is able to establish you by my gospel and the proclamation of Jesus Christ, according to the revelation of the mystery hidden for ages past but now revealed and made known through the prophetic writings by the command of the eternal God, so that all nations might believe and obey Him. (Rom. 16:25-26)

Remember Jesus Christ, raised from the dead, descended from David. This is my gospel. (2 Tim. 2:8)

I have become its servant by the commission God gave me to present to you the word of God in its fulness, the mystery that has been kept hidden for ages and generations, but it is now disclosed to the saints. (Col. 1:26)

These scriptures make it very clear that Paul had something special from the Lord for the church. Therefore it might be well for the church to understand what it is in the gospel of Paul.

Paul's conversion and revelation was about two years after the day of Pentecost. Jesus Christ called Paul to be an apostle of grace to the children of Israel and then to the Gentiles (Acts 9:15). The church today has a mixed message of law and grace. This is causing confusion among believers and stunt their growth in Christ. Those of us who are born again are part of the new creation whether they be Jew or Gentile. Jesus fulfilled the law the prophets and the covenants. Our faith is based on the finished work of Jesus Christ. He is the author and the finisher of our faith. We are from before the foundation of the world, chosen in Christ Jesus (Eph. 1:4). We were co-crucified with Christ, buried with Christ and on the third day we arose with Christ. When we believed in the Son of God that the Father raised him from the dead, Christ the person, spirit and life came into us and lives in us as us. We are complete in him (Col. 2:10). The Holy Spirit is revealing the truth to us more and more daily. As we behold Jesus who is in us we shall be changed from glory to glory and Christ is able to express himself through us spontaneously in his love for others nature. Paul says if any man or an angel from heaven come and preach another gospel, that we should let him be accursed (Gal. 1:8-9). Doing anything within ourselves of our own effort is religion compared to Christ working through us. God no longer accept man's work, but the work of his Son through the man. The blessing of knowing that the Lord of Life and resurrection lives in you is that you are free from any condemnation and fear of Satan. The mystery of the gospel according to Paul is Christ in you the hope of glory (Col. 1:27) which is a guarantee of an unbroken fellowship with the Lord.

> *We are united with the Lord and one with Him in spirit.*
> *(1 Cor. 6:17)*

This is the present-day truth from Jesus Christ for his church.

Our identification with Christ

> *For Christ's love compels us, because we are convinced*
> *that one died for all, and therefore all died. (2 Cor. 5:14)*

This scripture clearly shows that we are identified with Christ. The first point of identification is that we must see ourselves dead in Christ on the cross. His death was our death. Jesus who knew no sin became sin for me and died. God saw his Son on the cross as being exactly as we were in spirit before our spirit birth.

> *God made Him who had no sin to be sin for us, so that in*
> *Him we might become the righteousness of God. (2 Cor. 5:21)*

Before believing on the Lord Jesus Christ, we were hopelessly bound by sin.

> *Therefore, just as sin entered the world through one man*
> *(Adam) and death through sin, and in this way death came to*
> *all men, because all sinned. (Rom. 5:12)*

At that time we were identified with the one man Adam.

> *Just as through the disobedience of the one man the many*
> *were made sinners, so also through the obedience of the one*
> *Man (Christ) the many will be made righteous. (Rom. 5:19)*

God's grace has enabled us a change in identity through the finished work of the cross and our belief in the Lord Jesus Christ. Our identification has been exchanged from Adam to Christ. Christ paid with his life so believers could be free from the old sin nature and be in union with him.

> *For if, by the trespass of one man, death reigned through that one man, how much more will those who receive God's abundant provision of grace and the gift of righteousness reign in life through the one Man, Jesus Christ. (Rom. 5:17)*

Because of our identification in Christ, God does not see us through our external manifestations. He sees us through the cross and his Son who is in us.

Our union with Christ:

Jesus said:

> *I am the vine; you are the branches. If a man remains in Me and I in him, he will bear much fruit; apart from Me you can do nothing. (John 15:5)*

> *I in them and You in me. May they be brought to complete unity to let the world know that you sent me and have loved them even as you have loved me. I have made you known to them, and will continue to make you known in order that the love you have for me may be in them and that I myself may be in them. (John 17:23, 26)*

> *We must rightly divide the word of truth. (2 Tim. 2:15)*

Paul says that this is the mystery that God the Father willed to make known, "Christ in you the hope of glory" (Col. 1:27). Paul was so committed to share the mystery of the final gospel to the church. Christ lives in the individual believer to be the expression of life. "And this is the testimony: God has given us eternal life, and this life is in the Son."

> *He who has the Son has life; he who does not have the Son of God does not have life. (1 John 5:11, 12)*

He that is joined to the Lord is one with Him in spirit. (1 Cor. 6:17)

The natural mind cannot understand the truth without the revelation of the Holy Spirit. The church of Jesus Christ is being built upon the revelation of Jesus Christ (Matt. 16:18). For the same reason, Paul prayed that the God of our Lord Jesus Christ, the glorious Father, may give you the spirit of wisdom and revelation so that you may know him better (Eph. 1:17). Christ is the all in all for us.

The principle of growth is from beginning to end Christ imparted. All the scriptures as the Word of God center in Christ. Same way, the begetting, the birth, and the growth are all related to Christ. From the start to finish and in between God's object is the imparting of Christ through the Word, by teaching, and the Holy Spirit working upon the Word and the teaching concerning Christ. To grow and mature in Christ, the believer must spend time in the Word of God so that the Holy Spirit may reveal more of the Christ in you.

So then, growth is a ministry of Christ through the Word, the teaching, and through prayer. Fellowship and communion with God through Jesus Christ is a requirement for the renewal of our mind. A renewed mind allows you to hear the voice of God more clearly, and Christ will be able to express through you more fully in his love for other's nature. Communion is waiting upon the Lord silently and being able to hear the voice of God. Communion with God is having a dialogue with God. Most people think of prayer as a one-way street. Communion is not prayer, bringing a list of endless requests to God, but entering into his rest.

Rightly dividing the truth

Study to shew thyself approved unto God, a workman that needeth not to be ashamed, rightly dividing the word of truth.
(2 Tim. 2:15)

We need to understand that scriptures present three interpretations of God's plan. A single scripture could have three meanings to it. The first one is the *primary* strategic meaning at the time and place of its writing. The second is the *prophetic* meaning in which the scripture can mean something relates to the future. For example, in Psalm 22, David talks about the very scene of Calvary, so that it was pertinent to David at the time in his day that the psalm also prophetically describes things that will happen on Calvary. The third one is the *practical* meaning. All of the scriptures are good for practical application to believers. (2 Tim. 3:16). When you study the Bible, be careful to see what is said and to whom it is written. Promises given to Israel, an earthly people, are not for the new creation believers as a heavenly people. Believers were placed in Christ on the day of Pentecost. The believers are in Christ. The gospel of grace was given to Paul in the Arabian Desert. Paul's gospel is more important to the birthed in Christ with the Father's incorruptible seed (1 Pet. 1:23).

Communion with God

Come to Me, all you who are weary and burdened, and I will give you rest. (Matt. 11:28)

Be still (let go, relax, do not strive) and know that I Am God. (Ps. 46:10, translation added)

Knowing that Jesus has finished the work, and seated at the right hand of the Father, we can enter into his rest. Our God is a holy God. He is pure light and lives in an unapproachable light. God is self-existing, eternal, and the creator of the entire universe. He created everything for his pleasure. He created mankind in his image to have fellowship with him. God in his ever-flowing love opened his door wide through Jesus Christ so that unholy man can come and fellowship with him through Jesus Christ. Our God is an awesome God. The Godhead (The Father, The Son, and The Holy Spirit) always had fellowship in unity and in purpose in eternity and now God has invited us (whosoever will, Jew and Gentile alike) to join him in fellowship. Jesus prayed while on earth:

All of them may be one, Father, just as you are in me and I am in you. May they also be in us so that the world may believe that you have sent me. (John 17:20-22)

God's desire from the beginning was to dwell in a tabernacle that was not made by man.

Our fellowship is with the Father and His Son Jesus Christ.
(1 John 1:3)

Fellowship is soaking in the presence of the Lord. It is beholding the Lord, loving him and being loved, knowing that we are accepted in the beloved Son of God, based on the finished work of Christ on Calvary.

As we behold Him we shall be changed from glory to glory.
(2 Cor. 3:18)

We can commune with God at any time at any place. God himself has made a dwelling place for him within us in Christ. We worship him in the Holy of Holies within our spirit where he is seated. There we commune with him. Because Jesus Christ is Omnipresent, he can be in heaven and in us all at the same time. As we spend time in his presence, our old mind will be transformed to the mind of Christ and be delivered from the lust of the flesh, the lust of the eye, and the pride of life. We will become matured sons of God, and Christ will be able to fully manifest through us.

Jesus said:

Yet a time is coming and has come now when the true worshipers will worship the Father in spirit and truth, for they are the kind of worshipers the Father seeks. (John 4:23)

Therefore since we have a great High Priest who has gone into heaven, Jesus the Son of God, let us hold firmly to the faith we profess. For we do not have a High Priest who is unable to sympathize with our weakness, but we have one who has been tempted in every way, just as we are yet was without sin. Let us then approach the throne of grace with confidence, so that we may receive mercy and find grace in time of our need. (Heb. 4:14-16)

Be still and know that I Am God. (Ps. 46:10)

Be still, relax, let go, and do not strive. Just focus on the Lord of glory.

Quiet yourself. Physical and mental calmness is necessary for hearing the voice of God.

Soft, Christ-centered music can be great help to calm yourself to meditate on the Lord.

Fellowship is always a two-way conversation.

Recognize God's voice as spontaneous still voice within you.

Thoughts from our mind is analytical.

Thoughts from our spirit's mind is spontaneous.

Biblical meditation combines analysis and spontaneity.

God speaks through visions and dreams.

Be still outwardly and inwardly to hear the voice of God.

Write down the flow of thoughts and the words that comes to your mind.

Those who wait upon the Lord shall renew their strength. They will soar on wings like eagles; they will run and not grow weary, they will walk and not be faint. (Isa. 40:31)

Communing with the Lord is like taking a walk with God the Father in the garden, in the cool of the day, and having a dialogue with him. Once again we are back in the Garden of God, free to live in his presence in Christ. Let us take time to commune with God. It is the most important thing we can do as far as the Father is concerned. As we enter into his rest, we learn more and more about him. As a result, our mind will be renewed and we are able to hear from the Lord more clearly and the Lord will be able to express himself through us freely and spontaneously in his love nature to the world around us. The more we know Him, the deeper we grow into him and become less attracted to the world. We become more conscious of our position in heaven and become one with the purpose of God in this world. We will not selfishly go after the things God can give us but after God himself. Then the full power of his love will be manifested through us in the world. Then we understand what it is that the scripture says, "To be conformed to the likeness of His Son." To begin the process, it is very important to enter into his rest and feed upon his life. It is a journey from:

> *My beloved is mine and I am His.* to
> *I am my beloved's and my beloved is mine.* to
> *I am my beloved's and His desire is mine.*
> *(Song of Solomon 2:16, 6:13, 7:10; author's translation)*

Chapter 11

The Christian Pilgrimage

Therefore if anyone is in Christ, he is a new creation; the old has gone, the new has come. (2 Cor. 5:17)

The first thing any believer needs to know and understand is "who we are in Christ" and realize it and be able to apply it in our lives.

There are many scriptures in the letters of Paul, referring to our "in Christ" position. The above scripture speaks to us that at the new birth, all things have become completely new. The Word of God confirms that we have the person (Gal. 2:20), spirit (Rom. 8:9), nature (2 Pet. 1:4), and life of Christ (1 John 5:11-12). We have received all these at the time of the new birth from the incorruptible seed that we received (1 Pet. 1:23). We have now a shared life in Christ. We are a completely new race of people that never existed before. Adam's race was put to death in Christ on the cross. Our heritage is connected to Christ, who is the head of this new creation race of people. We are joined to Christ in this new creation race of people, chosen in Christ before the foundation of the world (Eph. 1:4). The old satanic nature of the spirit is completely wiped clean by the placing of God's seed of Christ in us at the time of our new birth. The spirit rebirthing salvation is a one-time event that happens instantaneously. But our mind is being progressively renewed by the Holy Spirit. Therefore, the old things of the mind are *being renewed* and it is a continuing process. It is important to know the difference. We have a part in the mind-renewing process by understanding first of all who we are now, in Christ Jesus. Secondly, we must begin to fellowship with the Word of God by meditating in it daily. As we meditate, we begin to develop a love relationship with the Christ who is in us. When our love relationship becomes more and more intense, we begin to lose interest in the fleshly activities of pleasing ourselves. The communion with God through Jesus Christ, who is our life, brings us to maturity as sons of God. The more mature we become the more we are interested in the will and the purpose of God in the church, the body of believers, as well as in the world. We are no longer focused on, "What is in it for me?" But rather we are focused on, "What is in it for God?" After all, God created all things, including mankind, for *his pleasure and for his glory.* Since we are sons of God, we too are invited to share in God's glory in Christ.

We do not have to be concerned about what is in it for us, because God has taken care of all our concerns. Let us look into some of the scriptures that point us to this truth.

1. All spiritual blessings in the heaven lies in Christ (Eph. 1:3).
2. All the promises of God to the new-birthed sons of God are in Christ.

    All the promises of God are Yes and in Him Amen, to the glory of God through us. (2 Cor. 1:20)

    Because we are birthed sons and not a covenant son like Israel, all the promises are to the sons of God in Christ.
3. The Father has placed all the fulness of Truth in Christ.

For it pleased the Father that in Him should all the fulness dwell. (Col. 1:19)

The Father's plan was that all fulness be found in Christ. For this reason, we do not have to go anywhere but in Christ who is in us for every need we might have. If it is not in Christ, then it is not a part of the eternal plan of God for the church.

4. We are complete in Christ the head with the fulness of the Trinity.

Paul writes:

For in Him dwells all the fulness of the Godhead bodily. (Col. 2:9) When we received Christ, we received the Godhead in Christ. We are complete in Him, who is the head of all principality and power. (Col. 2:10)

I have often wondered about Christian's preoccupation with Satan. We know that Satan is real, and I am not underestimating him. However, the truth is that:

Greater is He who is in us than he that is in the world. (1 John 4:4)

We need to understand that we have the head of all principality and power living in us. It is Christ in us who is our life, who has already defeated Satan.

For you died, and your life is hid with Christ in God. (Col. 3:3)

It means union with or oneness with Christ.

5. In Christ are hid all the treasures of wisdom and knowledge. Paul declares that the full riches of all knowledge and all the treasures of wisdom and knowledge are hidden in Christ (Col. 2:2, 3).

Our Father provides us His will and direction. The Holy Spirit renews our mind, so that the same mind of Christ will be in us. (Phil. 2:5)

The Holy Spirit also reveals to us that our wisdom righteousness sanctification and redemption, is all in Christ (1 Cor. 1:30).

6. The Holy Spirit is the teacher and revealer of this Christ who is in us.
    The Holy Spirit teaches the truth to the hungry hearts, who desires to know the Lord more and more and willing to search the scriptures diligently. These truths are not for

babies who are satisfied to be spoon fed by the preachers once a week.

> *I pray that the God of our Lord Jesus Christ, the Father of glory may give you the spirit of wisdom and revelation in the knowledge of Him. (Eph. 1:17)*

Only by revelation of the Holy Spirit you are able to see that every answer to your question will be revealed to be in Christ.

7. The mystery of the Father's will is in Christ.
    Christ is our life, our strength, our fullness, and our all. The Father wants each one of us to know the mystery of his will which he purposed in Christ Jesus. In the fullness of times, the Father is gathering to bring all things in heaven and on earth under one head, even Christ (Eph. 1:10).

> *God always causes us to triumph in Christ. (2 Cor. 2:14)*

God placed all things under his feet and appointed him to be head over everything for the Church, which is His body, the fullness of Him who fills everything in every way (Eph. 1:22, 23).

8. Christ will reveal the Father to us. The believer's walk is by the spirit in him and not by rules, regulations, and commands. The believer is dead, and Christ lives in his place (Gal. 2:20). The believer lives by another life, Christ himself is this life. You are also in Christ and therefore alive to God (Rom. 6:11).

Just as the Father was in Christ and Christ in the Father during his earthly ministry, now Christ is in us and we are also in Christ. Jesus said, "I can do nothing on my own, I say only that which I hear the Father say and I only do that which I see the Father do" (John 14:10). We have a speaking Lord within us and we hear his voice deep within us. Therefore, we too must speak only what we hear from the Lord and do what we see the Lord does in our walk in the spirit. It is the Lord in us who desires to express unconditional love to others through us. We are the earthen vessel that contains the treasure from the other realm. The Christian life must be lived by Christ in us. For this reason, the Father sent his Son to live in us. The Father is pleased in his beloved Son and see him in us and accepted us and also pleased with us. The mystery of God is Christ in us. Our fellowship is with the Father and his Son, the Lord Jesus Christ. As we continue with the internal fellowship with our Lord, we are able to fellowship with one another and share with, care for, and bear with the fellow believers.

Christ is all and in all

Christ is the all in all for every believer at the new birth. Christ is the express image of the Father in every part of his character and essence.

> *Who being the radiance of glory and the express image of His essence, and supporting all things by the word of His power.*
> *(Heb. 1:3a)*

The spoken word of Christ supports and sustains everything and every one in creation. When we received Christ at the spirit birth, we also received the Father and the Holy Spirit. Paul says that in Christ "dwells all the fullness of Godhead bodily" (Col. 2:9). Now we are the body of Christ and members in particular (1 Cor. 12:27).

We are called the body of Christ and not the body of the Holy Spirit. It is Christ who is being expressed in and through us to others. The Holy Spirit "will teach you all things" (John 14:26). The Holy Spirit will guide you *into all truth* (John 16:13). The Holy Spirit will take all things that the Father has given to the Son and declare it to you (John 16:15). The Holy Spirit, the Spirit of Truth, has come to teach us of all things of the Son, who is the Person of Truth (John 14:6). The reality of Christian life comes when the Holy Spirit transforms the mind of the believer to the revelation that Christ lives in us. Christ lives in the many membered bodies at the present time. At the time of the spirit birth, we presented ourselves to God, and we need to continually do so in order that the Holy Spirit may transform us by encouraging us to choose the mind of Christ in us. The Spirit of Christ in us is a love for other's spirit. Love is opposite to self. Christ lives in us through his love for other's life as us unto the Father as our all in all. When Christ starts living and expressing himself spontaneously through us, the Christ in us will begin to reveal the Father in us.

John said:

Truly our fellowship is with the Father and with His Son Jesus Christ. (John 1:3)

Paul said:

It is no longer I who live, but Christ lives in me. (Gal. 2:20)

Therefore, Christ is all in all in me.

Be transformed by the renewing of your mind (Rom. 12:2)

The born-again believer's spirit is perfected by Christ who is in us. However, the soul of the believer which consists of mind, will, and emotion is unchanged at the time of our birthing. The soul of the believer with its sin nature still wants to run its own show of pleasing self. The soul is now opposed to the new spirit in Christ. The mind of the believer needs to be brought under the obedience of the spirit. This is called spiritual growth. However, it is not the spirit that is growing, but it brings the soul under the control of the spirit. There must be some adjustments made in our mind, will, and emotion so that the Christ life can be expressed through the mind. The goal is for us to be in the image of Christ in all things to grow up in him who is the head, that is, Christ. Each believer has to go through the transformation of the soul. We all need to reach unity in faith and in the knowledge of the Son of God and become mature, attaining to the full measure of Christ (Eph. 4:13).

This is an ongoing process throughout the Christian life on earth. This world is a schoolhouse, where we learn how to live in the Father's house. The Father desires many sons in the divine nature of the Only Begotten Son Jesus Christ. Our attitude must be the same as that of Christ. God will take care of it in his own way. God deals with each one of us in a different way. God will change us through adverse circumstances and situations, trials and tribulations. Our flesh likes to hide deep in the darkness and does not want to be exposed to the light of God, because it does not want to give up its own way of self preservation. God's pruning knife comes in many fashions. It usually comes as an answer to our prayers for transformation and willingness to a complete surrender to God's will.

The Christian life is not a bed of roses.

> *For it has been granted to you on behalf of Christ not only to believe on Him, but also to suffer for Him. (Phil. 1:29)*

Why Christians Suffer?

Suffering is the way to transformation. We are partakers of the divine nature. That means, we need to share in his sufferings also just as we share in his love. Many Christians wonder about the sufferings they go through in life. It is unfortunate that Christians are mislead to believe that they suffer because of their sin or due to lack of their faith in God. I cannot agree with this kind of thinking because the Bible is full of stories about adverse circumstances and suffering. I personally have experienced many trials and tribulations and still do. I thank my God for the trials that came my way which allowed me to change from self-love to loving others first. I am not saying that in any way I am perfect but God continuously bringing up the darkness of my soul to light through various circumstances. However, unfair it may appear to me, it works for his purpose in me and for me to change from glory to glory.

Let us look at some of the examples God has given us to learn from them.

The story of Job in the Bible tell us about Job's suffering. God himself said that Job was a righteous man. Therefore, the sickness and the calamities did not come because of sin. The story clearly shows that in the end Job was changed. Job says:

My ears had heard of you but now my eyes have seen you. Therefore I despise my self and repent in dust and ashes. (Job 42:5)

Job came to *know* God through his trial and was changed for the better.

Abraham had to leave his city, his gods, and his family and go to an unknown place God promised him.

Abraham had to wait patiently for twenty-five years before the promise of the son fulfilled. Abraham had to get rid of his son Ismael, who came without the promise through Hagar. That was emotionally painful for a father. More than that when Isaac had to be offered as a sacrifice at the command of God, did he not emotionally suffer? Oh yes! The end result was that Abraham came to know his God and was changed. Abraham believed God and was counted as righteousness to him. Abraham became father of many nations as promised by God. The world was blessed through Jesus Christ whose human ancestory come from Abraham. God of the bible is known as the God of Abraham, Isaac and Jacob.

Joseph became the right hand man of Pharoah in Egypt but did he go through some unfair treatment?

Joseph shared a dream with his brothers and they hated him for that and tried to kill him, then decided to sell to an Egyptian. Then Pontipher's wife falsely accused him of rape and he was sent to prison. Joseph stayed in the Egyptian dungeon for thirteen years for no fault of his own. Was it fair? God dealt with him for thirteen years. Joseph was changed. When he was promoted as the right man of pharoah, Joseph was able to forgive his brothers and said, "What you meant for evil God made it for good."

David, Israel's greatest king and the sweet Psalmist, was chased by King Soul for thirteen years to kill him. David had to hide in caves and run all over Israel to escape the sword of Soul. Another time David ended up in a Philistine jail, to cover his identity he had to fake madness. Had the Philistines known the true identity as David who killed Goliath, they would have killed him right there. David also suffered greatly at the death of his son Absalom. His sorrows and sufferings are written in the book of Psalms. David also suffered at the death of his son through Bedshebah. David had changed through all the sufferings. David became known to be "the man after God's own heart." David reigned as king of Israel for forty years and conquered all the land that was promised to Israel. Jesus's human ancestry comes from the house of David. God made a covenant with David that the throne of his kingdom will be everlasting.

Let us look at Jesus Christ

Jesus Christ came to this world leaving all the glory with his Father in heaven to be born as a man. He did not have a place to be born in this earth. He was despised and rejected by his own people Israel. He was falsely accused by the religious leaders and said that he was doing the miracles by the power of the Devil. He came as Israel's Messiah but was rejected first by the Jewish leaders and then by the nation of Israel. He received the thirty-nine lashes by the Roman soldiers on his back. They arrested him like a common criminal. He was ridiculed, slapped, and spat upon by sinful men. Retaliation never entered his mind. The agony he went through at Gethsemane, no man can describe. "Crucify him," they cried. The horrible death on the cross, no man can understand. Seeing the joy set before him, he endured the cross. Was it fair for him to suffer? The one who knew no sin?

> *During the days of Jesus on earth, He offered up prayers and petitions with loud cries and tears to the one who could save Him from death, and He was heard because of His reverent submission. Although He was a Son, He learned obedience from what He suffered and, once made perfect, He became the source of eternal salvation for all who obey Him and was designated but God to be High Priest in the order of Melchizedek. (Heb. 5:7-10)*

Jesus suffered, because he loved the world. We fellowship in his suffering because we love him and through him we also love the world as ambassadors of Christ.

What about Paul the apostle? Did he not suffer? Paul's trials and tribulations in his own words:

I have worked much harder, been in prison more frequently, been flogged more severely, and been exposed to death again and again. Five times I received from the Jews the forty lashes minus one. Three times I was beaten with rods, once I was stoned, three times I was ship wrecked, I spent a night and day in the open sea, I have been constantly on the move. I have been in danger from rivers, in danger from bandits in danger from my own country men, in danger from Gentiles; in danger in the city, in danger in the country, in danger from false brothers. I have labored and toiled and often gone without sleep; I have known hunger and thirst and have often gone without food; I have been cold and naked. Besides everything else, I face daily the pressure of my concern for all the churches. Who is weak, and I do not feel weak? Who is led into sin, I do not inwardly burn? (2 Cor. 11:23-29)

Paul's answers for these trials:

1. "And He died for all, that those who live should no longer live for themselves but for Him who died for them and was raised again." (2 Cor. 4:15)
2. "Therefore, we do not lose heart. Though we outwardly are wasting away, yet inwardly we are being renewed day by day. For our *light and momentary troubles* are achieving for us an *eternal glory* that far outweighs them all. So we fix our eyes not on what is seen, but on what is unseen. For what is seen is temporary, but what is unseen is eternal" (2 Cor. 4:16-18).
3. "And we know that in all things God works for good for those who love him, who have been called according to His purpose. For those God foreknew, he also predestined to be conformed to the likeness of his Son,

that He might be the firstborn among many brothers" (Rom. 8:28-29).
4. Who shall separate us from the love of Christ? Shall trouble or hardship or persecution or famine or nakedness or danger or sword "No, in all these things, we are more than conquerors through Him who loved us. For I am convinced that neither death nor life, neither angels nor demons, neither the present nor the future, nor any powers, neither height nor depth, nor anything else in all creation, will be able to separate us from the love of God that is in Christ Jesus our Lord" (Rom. 8:35-39).
5. "Now I rejoice in what was suffered for you, and I fill up in my flesh what is still lacking in regard to Christ's afflictions, for the sake of His body, which is the church. I have become its servant by the commission God gave me to present to you the word of God in its fullness the mystery that has been kept hidden for ages, but is now disclosed to the saints. To them, God has chosen to make known among the Gentiles the glorious riches of this mystery, which is Christ in you the hope of glory" (Col. 1:24-27).
6. "But whatever was to my profit I now consider them loss for the sake of Christ. I want to *know Christ* and the power of His resurrection and the fellowship of sharing in His sufferings, becoming like Him in His death, and so somehow, to attain to the resurrection from the dead" (Phil. 3:7, 10).
7. "Let your gentleness be evident to all. The Lord is near. Do not be anxious about anything, but in everything, by prayer and petition with thanksgiving, present your requests to God. And the peace of God, which transcends all understanding, will guard your hearts and minds in Christ Jesus" (Phil. 4:5-7).

Our citizenship is in heaven. We are pilgrims on this earth. Everything that happens to us comes from the hand of God. Our heavenly Father disciplines us because we are his children and he has a plan for us to prosper and not to harm us. When we accept this truth, then our life will be better for it.

Chapter 12

My personal experience of the grace of God

Blessed be the God and Father of our Lord Jesus Christ, the Father of mercies and God of all comfort who comforts us in all our tribulation, that we may be able to comfort those who are in any trouble, with the comfort with which we ourselves are comforted by God. For as the sufferings of Christ abound in us, so our consolation also abounds through Christ. (2 Cor. 1:3)

    I was born in the southern part of India in a Christian home by the grace of God. Our families have been Christians for almost 2000 years. We believe that we are the converts of Apostle Thomas's disciples. The apostle came to southern India in AD 52 according to the church history. He built seven churches in South India. Some of those churches still exist to this day. The church is of Syrian Orthodox Denomination. It is a mixture of Judaism, Catholicism, and Protestantism. Salvation is not clearly preached or understood. Even then God is working for the benefit of his people.

    Good works and keeping the law is the way to heaven. Needless to say that I did not have a personal relationship with the Lord Jesus at the time. We believed in Jesus Christ, and going to church every Sunday morning and evening was the way of life. I remember that in the village, after the sunset, at every house, there is singing and praying. Christians prayed to their God, Hindus to their god, and Muslims to their god. We all coexisted as a community, helping each other and caring for each other. I never knew atheists until I came to the West. I thought everyone believed in some god of their choice.

When I was twelve years old, one evening as I was going to the neighbor, barefoot, I was bitten by a snake. I knew something bit me. Since it was nighttime I could not make out what it was, but I remember shaking it off my left foot and calling for my father. My father immediately tried to milk the blood from the site. There were two tooth marks between my toes. By midnight, the pain became intense and climbing gradually to my foot and then to my leg. My family did not take me to the hospital because the hospital was far and no transportation was available at the time. We were in a small village surrounded by farmland. My parents and my grandmother prayed. I talked to the Lord and said, "Lord Jesus, please do not take me now because if died tonight, I am not sure that I will go to heaven because I lied yesterday to my father about my homework. Please take me when I am sure that I am going to heaven." About two o'clock, even with the pain, I fell asleep. I woke up in the morning and found myself alive. I was well except for a heavily swollen foot. It was Sunday and I walked with my family to church, which was about three miles away. By the grace of God, I lived, and three days later, my father killed the cobra in the same place when it came out of its hiding place.

When I was studying in Bombay, I happened to jump into a train that was beginning to move and fell under the train. I could hear the people making a lot of commotion from the platform, thinking about a young girl who they thought to be mutilated or dead. Once the train went away, I put my hand up and they pulled me out and there was not even a scratch on my body. I took the next train and went on to do what I was going to do. I could almost hear a still voice saying to me, "I have a plan for you to prosper and not to harm you." Once again God's grace kept me from any harm.

Some years later, I met my husband in Bombay, and after the marriage, I moved to the Netherlands, where my husband came from. The transition was the biggest trial for me and had a difficult time in adjusting to the climate, food, different people, and strange language. Soon I found out that my husband and his family did not go to church or believed in God. They were wonderful people, very caring and loving. I was terribly disappointed and wondered what I got myself into. Reading was my recreation, and I spent a lot of time in the Dutch Library. I checked out few English books they had to take with me. Among those books, there was one titled, *The cross and the switchblade* by David Wilkerson. I met Jesus Christ through that book. From that time on, I prayed that God may allow me to come to America so that I can meet with Mr. Wilkerson because I had a lot of questions. Soon after that, my husband said to me that we are going to America. Of course, he knew nothing of my prayer. I was delighted and worked very hard in preparation to come to America. We saved up some money for financial freedom, in case we cannot find jobs right away.

We came to the United States in 1975 with a three-year-old child. In the beginning, it was very hard for all of us. With faith in God and through hard work, we overcame the many difficulties of settling in a new country.

I found a church nearby and started to go there and made some friends. God gave me such hunger for the Word of God, and soon I was buying Christian books in large numbers and started studying the bible on my own. I continued to work as registered nurse at one of the hospitals in town. I saw the scripture early on in John 2:27:As for you, the anointing you received from Him remains in you, and you do not need anyone to teach you. But as His anointing teaches you about all things and as that anointing is real, not counterfeit-just as it has taught you, remain in Him.

In 1989 I was having a lot of pain in my stomach and the doctors could not find what was wrong with me for about six months. In the end, the diagnosis they made was cancer of the stomach (adenocarcinoma).

The mortality rate was almost 100 percent. The doctors decided to do surgery right away and removed most of my stomach. During those days, I heard the voice of God clearly and my Lord walked me through the whole process. He comforted me with scriptures everyday. God provided me with wonderful support system of family friends and my church family. After surgery, I came home and the doctors wanted me to take massive dose of chemotherapy after a week for six months. The Lord showed me clearly that I was not to take chemotherapy. I made the decision not to take chemotherapy and my husband agreed with me which was very surprising because he was still an unbeliever. The doctors told my husband that I might live for six months. My Son was getting ready to go to college during the fall, which was an added emotional pain for me, to think that our only child is leaving home. God took care of all his needs as well. My husband and our son both suffered with me. After my recovery from surgery about six weeks later, I started working again. By the grace of God, I continued to prosper in health. I became more close to the Lord than ever before. Sometimes when I was alone, I wondered if I was truly healed of the cancer. I used to ask the Lord for scriptures for confirmation of my healing. The Lord faithfully gave me scriptures to support that I was healed. Few weeks later, when I asked the Lord for another scripture, he said, "My child, I would like you to go to Egypt with me when Israel was delivered from their slavery in Egypt." He asked me to narrate the story of the last plague. I told the story how Moses instructed the people to kill the Lamb and apply the blood of the Lamb on their door posts so that the death angel will pass over them and their firstborns will be spared from death. At that moment, the Lord said in a loud voice, "If the animals' blood caused the death angel to pass over, how much more having sprinkled your heart with my blood the death angel has to pass you over?" I was so overwhelmed by the presence of the Lord and said in a trembling voice, "Lord, please forgive me for my unbelief." The Lord knew I had the fear of death, and he settled that issue right there. I never had to ask for conformation of my healing anymore. This is the reason that I chose the title of the book, *The Blood of The Lamb of God*. During this time, God showed me that Christ Jesus lived in me (Gal. 2:20) and I lived in him and he is my healer and the all in all for me.

For in Him we live and move and have our being. (Acts 17:28)

For you died, and your life is hidden with Christ in God. (Col. 3:3)

To me, this message was the most liberating from all condemnations and fear. When the Lord sets you free, you shall be free indeed. Hallelujah!

I continued to be in good health until 2001 January when I found out that I had breast cancer. Once again I had to go through surgery (mastectomy). The doctors recommended to take chemotherapy as an adjunct treatment. I prayed again and did not want to take the chemotherapy, but my husband and my son wanted me to go through it. My son and his wife were expecting their first baby and they all wanted me to be around. The Lord said that it was my choice and that either way I will be all right. So I decided to go through the chemotherapy, which was a very rough road. Again by the grace of God, I lived through it with the help of family and friends. Once I recovered from all the therapy, I went back to work and continued to be in good health.

In 2003 my husband became a believer in Christ. This was one of the best things that happened to us.

My son and my daughter-in-love are raising their children in the ways of God. I am overwhelmed by God's grace toward me. What an awesome God we worship and his love endures forever! All I can say is that:

> *Bless the Lord O my soul and all that is within me, Bless His Holy Name. Bless the Lord O my soul and forget not all His benefits; who forgave all my sins and healed all my diseases; who has delivered me from destructions and crowned me with loving kindness and tender mercies; satisfied my mouth with good things and my youth is renewed like an eagle's. (Ps. 103:1-5)*

I did not deserve any of God's favor, but my Father in heaven blessed me with his grace in the person of Jesus Christ. All these blessings and more are available to everyone of you. His grace is always sufficient to overcome all the difficulties in life. He is more than enough for all of us if you know him. We must seek him diligently. He must be first in every area of your life without wavering.

In the meantime, I started studying the Bible seriously by enrolling in a Bible school. Here I am. It is 2010. I am doing well, and the goodness and mercy of the Lord follows me. I finished my Bible studies and earned the degree of doctorate in theology. But it is the fellowship I have with my Lord is what I cherish. Every moment that I am awake, I stay in touch with the Lord. For many months, God was speaking to me about this book and how to put it all together, and now is the time. I trust in the Lord that I was able to encourage or comfort someone through these words of my experience with the grace of my Father in heaven who loves us so dearly through his Son Jesus Christ.

I pray that you too will come to know the Father's love and enjoy the freedom in the spirit, knowing who you are in Christ Jesus, and enter into his rest (Isa. 30:15).

"To Him who sits on the throne and unto the Lamb be blessing and honor and glory and power forever and ever! Amen!"

A. Elizabeth Verbeek

Edwards Brothers, Inc.
Thorofare, NJ USA
June 28, 2011